Glyn Marston, an asbestos surveyor by profession and a man with numerous achievements in ultra-distance running to his name, was forced to retire from running due to a serious knee injury but found a new pastime on two wheels. Long-distance cycling became his new passion and the joys of taking on challenges in the Audax UK calendar was to give him the joy he once had in ultra-distance running.

The Paris-Brest-Paris cycling event is a huge challenge in the Audax cycling calendar – will Glyn be successful in his attempt to qualify?

Angie Marston, my ever-supportive wife.

3CJ Cycle Centre in Longbridge – Clint, Dennis and Andy – for keeping me on two wheels.

Vanessa Morris, Cycling UK, for the encouragement.

Cannon Hill Cycling Club, for the great training sessions.

Freddie Mercury, for inspiring the challenge.

Glyn Marston

FINDING FREDDIE: THE (ALTERNATIVE) PARIS–BREST–PARIS STORY

AUSTIN MACAULEY PUBLISHERS™

LONDON • CAMBRIDGE • NEW YORK • SHARJAH

A CIP catalogue record for this title is available from the British Library.

ISBN 9781398407558 (Paperback)
ISBN 9781398416246 (ePub e-book)

www.austinmacauley.com

First Published (2021)
Austin Macauley Publishers Ltd
25 Canada Square
Canary Wharf
London
E14 5LQ

To Austin Macauley for their wonderful assistance and help in bringing this book to life.

Introduction

The Paris–Brest–Paris 2015 had been a disappointment for me as I failed to complete the course due to a knee injury and with medics suggesting that I pulled out of the event; I retired from the race with huge regret.

The Paris–Brest–Paris (PBP) is staged once every four years and I would have to carry the burden of regret until 2019, when I would get another chance.

A lot had happened in my life since 2015, I had married a wonderful woman named Angela – or Angie, as she prefers to be called.

I was working for a great company as an Asbestos surveyor and commanding a great wage too, because of my extensive experience and knowledge.

2016 was the year that Angie and I got married, and with that came a barrage of abusive messages to Angie from a female stalker that I had; this woman was intent on breaking us up, but thankfully, and after a lengthy expensive legal battle, she was forced to leave us alone (that is another story though).

For the first time in years, I was in the frame of mind that I was in when I was running distances of 150 miles, taking on longer distance running events and succeeding.

I could no longer run, but I had two wheels and I was feeling that it was time to hit the roads and prove to myself that I still had it in me, and with the support and encouragement from Angie, I couldn't fail...or could I?

My story starts towards the end of 2018.

Chapter One

Bloody Work!

After a few years of working for a great company, I was unaware of the huge changes that were ahead of myself and my colleagues; the company I was working for had merged with another company and with that came some huge changes in company policy – changes for the worse from an employee's point of view.

The first sign of trouble was evident as my manager had quit his post suddenly and with no goodbyes to anyone, almost as if he were whisked away somewhere else without any higher management talking of his leaving.

Then came a huge blow to all asbestos surveyors who were out in the field or out on sites. Our company credit cards were withdrawn and we had to pay our own expenses and claim the money back at the end of each month, this would be a huge blow to anyone working in (or around) London – with parking fees being anything up to £30 a day and having to pay for your own meals (including breakfast); the week would be very expensive.

With the departure of my manager, I was to see a new manager promoted to the position and thankfully, a man I considered a friend (or was he?).

The new manager (over a period of time) seemed to enjoy sitting in his office and waiting for work to come to him, instead of going out there to get work in; this resulted in a few of us working away a lot and working for other regional offices around the UK.

I could never understand why my (new) manager was claiming that there was not enough work for our office and that was why I was working away from home a lot. Yet, he was setting on new trainees? This was later proven as a cost cutting exercise, to take on trainees and pay peanuts and try to put us, more experienced asbestos surveyors, in a position where we would feel that we would have to quit our jobs. The current situation was to save the company a lot of money over the year, and with myself and some other colleagues not willing to sign up to a new contract that would see us working weekends without being given prior notice, it was clear that our time with the company would be coming to an end.

I did enjoy working in Devon, Dorset and Cornwall because I would pack my bike in the van and cycle after work rather than sit alone in my hotel room; the work I was doing would see me finish for the day at 2 pm most days and I would rush back to my hotel room to get changed into my cycling gear.

I was putting in some high mileage on my bike and my training was coming along great for the plans ahead and those plans were to see me qualify for the Paris–Brest–Paris 2019.

My Strava segments were improving greatly (this being prolific stretches of roads on the Strava website). But things began to take a turn for the worse when my manager gave a job to someone with a chequered past; this new starter had worked for a couple of asbestos surveying companies over the previous year but he had never gained his P.402 certificate (it is needed to be allowed to conduct asbestos surveys – a proof of competency within the industry).

This new starter was working with me and it was my role to train him and get him ready for his P.402 course, however, his behaviour on site was worrying and at times was risking my own well-being (such as walking away when he should have been footing a ladder – a ladder that I was standing at the top of).

This guy would disappear when on site and be missing for hours, but I didn't mind because it allowed me to concentrate on my work while he was absent; his presence was that of chaos, unpredictability and total nonsense.

My suspicions of him became aroused when my head office requested that I make sure that this new starter had filled in his form for a DBS check (the new CRB check) and after a number of requests, I was informed to tell him that he would be disciplined if he didn't get this form filled in and sent to head office soon. Despite this, he still made excuses as to why he didn't fill it in, and so I asked the head office to use a copy of this guy's driving licence or a copy of his passport to make enquiries because I was certain that he was hiding something sinister and filling out a DBS form would have exposed his secret.

How horrified was I when head office told me that on his way to his three-day induction in Newcastle, he had lost his wallet on the train and along with it was his passport and the driving licence.

"So, you don't have any real proof of his identity nor do you have any proof that he can legally drive, but you are allowing him to drive a company van?" I asked.

The head office confirmed that my manager was instructed to allow this guy to drive only after he had produced his driving licence, but my manager gave him the benefit of the doubt and allowed him to drive anyway, without having first shown his driving licence. At this time, I refused to work with the guy until positive checks had been made surrounding the man and his background.

It turned out that this guy had convictions for shoplifting (mainly alcohol), a drug habit and assaulting a man and his wife. Because of the company's zero tolerance on drugs and alcohol, the guy was dismissed instantly and my manager was disciplined for being so negligent in this situation – of course the manager blamed me for his warning from the company which caused him great embarrassment.

After that came week after week of working nights along the cold and dark railway tracks in the middle of nowhere or working in London where I would be paying up to £30 a day for parking and then pay for my meals on top; my money was running out quick as I had to wait for payday to recoup my expenses. Of course, I couldn't take my bike to London because I wasn't totally confident that I could get a good training session with the city traffic.

Everything came to a head and I was threatening to take action for constructive dismissal on the basis that I was working away or more unsociable hours compared to other colleagues; this resulted in the company paying me a fee to walk away quietly and bring no action to the company – I accepted.

And so, a new start with a new company was soon offered and I was excited to be working so soon after finishing with my old company, but I was to find out that all was not what it seemed.

At my interview, I was told that I would be working on a Solihull contract, an area close to my home, but instead, I was working in Daventry and Stoke-on-Trent. It was the Stoke-on-Trent contract that was causing issues.

At this point, I will try and explain the types of asbestos surveys that are conducted.

1. Management surveys

A survey that is a visual inspection of a property with no intrusions or damage caused to the property and if a surveyor sees something that may contain asbestos, then that surveyor will take a sample and send it to the lab for testing.

Any areas that are not accessed can be referred to as a presumption (presuming that asbestos is likely to be in a location) or 'strongly' presume if there is strong evidence that an asbestos containing material is likely to be present.

2. Refurbishment/Demolition surveys

A survey that has all areas accessed, including cavity areas within walls and floor void areas and all roof areas (inside and out).

This kind of survey allows a surveyor to 'KNOCK THE CRAP' out of property to gain access to restricted areas, and because of this, it takes a lot longer to carry out than a 'Management' survey.

And so, in the Stoke contract, the client was paying for a management survey but wanted a refurbishment survey. The company I was now working for required seven or eight surveys a day to make the contract pay despite HSE (Health and Safety Executive) guidelines stating that no more than five management surveys a day should be conducted (six at a push).

We were being forced into rushing these jobs. There were long hours and constant arguing with office staff when I refused to take on extra work (I couldn't manage the workload I was already given, let alone take on more work); it was evident that I needed to leave. By this time, I was becoming anxious about the lack of personal time I was getting; the lack of time with my wife and the lack of time to continue my training for the 2019 PBP (Paris–Brest–Paris).

Okay, cycling doesn't pay the bills, but everyone deserves their own time out and work should not be allowed to take over the whole day (and evening). I left within a short time of working for this company.

So, in a short period, I was now working for another company and within a couple of weeks, I knew I had made a mistake but I had to stick with it until something better came along.

I was in a much worse position now as all of my work was around Buckinghamshire, Swindon, Bedfordshire and Central London.

Leaving my home at stupid o'clock in the morning every morning and getting home late in the evening made me feel like I was serving a prison sentence.

I would get in my van at 4:30 am and not get home until 7 pm on most days, tired and deflated. I would fall asleep on the settee only to be woken by Angie who would actually help me walk up the stairs to bed (fatigue was taking over my body so badly that I could barely manage the walk upstairs).

My focus on the PBP 2019 event was slipping away, I had to qualify and to qualify for the event, I needed to successfully complete a 200-km ride, 300-km ride, 400-km ride and a 600-km ride all before June 2019 and under the current circumstances, I was not going to make any of the qualifiers.

However, with the support of Angie, I was able to get on my exercise bike in the garage – not the best form of training but I have an innovative exercise bike that is used (apparently) by Tour de France cyclists, it's a bike that is powered by Google Maps and I can cycle anywhere in the world without leaving my home – this bike simulates uphills and downhills and gives you the feeling of real time cycling – and what makes it great is the fact that you cannot roll downhill on it (you keep pedalling even when the bike is in downhill position).

It wasn't the best way to train but it was better than doing nothing and as soon as I had warmed up, the tiredness in my body was removed for a while.

In some cases, I was cycling up to thirty miles an evening on this bike and with long distance cycling out on the roads at the weekends, I was praying that this would be just enough to get me through my first PBP qualifier in a few weeks' time.

My plan of events for the year – including qualifying for the PBP 2019, was:

February 2nd – 200-km (125-mile) Tewkesbury (PBP Qualifier)
March 16th – 300-km (186-mile) Tewkesbury (PBP Qualifier)
March 24th – 100-mile Mad March Hare – Birmingham.
April 7th – Bostin Chase 40-Mile (Accompanied by Angie)

April 27th – 400-km (248-mile) – Alfreton (PBP Qualifier)
May 12th – Birmingham Velo – 100-mile June 8th – 600-km (375-mile) Poynton, S of Stockport (PBP Qualifier).
August 4th – Ride London 100 miles (Accompanied by Angie)
August 18th–22nd – Paris–Brest–Paris (PBP) 1200-km (75-mile)

However, the week running up to my first qualifier was to be the worst week ever; longer hours and with the company issuing a statement that they may be stopping payment for driving to and from work sites. I became concerned because I would have to leave home earlier to make sure I was on site for 8 am but get home later as I would not be able to leave site until after 5 pm. I would be practically working sixteen-hour days for eight hours' pay.

And then came a suggestion in a company meeting, "We will be putting up a performance chart on the office wall, if you do your job as expected, you will get a tick, but if you do more than expected, you will get a plus tick. Do less than expected and you will get a minus tick."

"WHAT! Are we back at school now? What a stupid idea – you can't publicise work performance for individuals, it will lead to harassment and bullying – in fact, it is corporate bullying," I replied in disgust.

"It's to encourage a better work ethic in staff," was the response.

"No – it's to bully staff into doing more unpaid hours, it is evident that this company is penny pinching – you don't pay out individual expenses for things such as parking, tools that I had to buy for a 'one-off job' which is not going to be reimbursed – you have surveyors breaking HSE guidelines by taking work home and sitting up to midnight inputting work data so they can get the numbers up and keep the company off their back…and you want more?"

As I walked over to a huge 'A' frame Nobo easel that had a huge writing pad, I made a statement to the group that were sucking up to the management and at the same time I started writing on the pad. I called out, "Your idea of a performance chart on the office wall will result in one thing, it will…

Cause
Resentful
Attitudes among
People

Speaks for itself really, doesn't it?"

This didn't go down too well at all and so was the beginning of the end of my time with this company and this was becoming clear when I had jobs that I had to be at before 7 am and jobs that were booked for after 4 pm…in Luton, so again I was jumping in my van at 4:30 am and not getting home until after 7:30 pm – my patience was wearing thin as I realised that my day was being planned to completely wind me up.

And on Friday, the first of February 2019 (the day before my first PBP qualifier), things were going to get even more heated!

I was working in Swindon and instead of carrying out the usual six asbestos surveys for Swindon council, I had four properties to do.

I puzzled at why the easy day's work for a change but I was soon to find out – heavy snow had fallen in and around Swindon through the night and a thick layer of snow was laid on a bed of hidden ice; Swindon council didn't want any contractors working on any of their properties and my company was the only company who insisted on allowing me to work in the area. As I drove off the M5 and onto the A417/A419, it was as if I had crossed an invisible border into Narnia; the whole area was like a scene from *The Lion, the Witch and the Wardrobe* with everything covered in a blanket of white.

It was a beautiful scene but horrible to drive along and I was there to work and not to look at the views – it was going to be a bad day for me as I was already struggling to drive my van.

Swindon council were really concerned about my welfare and the now dangerous conditions that I was facing when driving in between sites.

I received a phone call from the council to inform me that they would be sending their own staff home early as police reported many, many car accidents and driving would not be an option for the day. After this, the council called my boss to request that he send me home as they did not want the thought of myself risking harm on their properties. And so, my boss called me.

"I have decided to send you home, mate," he said, "due to the weather conditions, I have a duty of care toward you and I want you home safely, but can you do me a job on the way home?"

"Yes, if it's on the way home, I can do it, I guess," I reluctantly replied.

"It's in Aylesbury – Wendover, to be exact," he explained.

"Wendover?" I replied in a shocked manner. "Wendover is two hours in the opposite direction to where I live. Can someone else do it?"

Apparently, a member of staff had called in sick and it was his job for the day – a job that needed to be done urgently.

I will admit that I wasn't happy with the situation as I was now contemplating a late finish again and with my first PBP qualifier the next day, I wanted to be home earlier if possible, and so, with the thought of getting home after 8 pm due to the weather conditions, I started to make my way to Wendover.

The roads out of Swindon were completely gridlocked as it seemed that every company in the area had allowed their staff to go home early, cars were sliding out of control at junctions and hitting stationary vehicles and the traffic became a standstill.

My sat-nav had taken me to the M4 and was to take me on the London-bound carriageway of the motorway, however, the motorway was jammed and a queue of standstill traffic had blocked the slip road onto the motorway.

I drove around aimlessly, trying to find an alternative way of getting to Wendover and with my sat-nav screaming at me to make my way to the M4. I was just ignoring it and hoping that soon, it would pick up an alternative route for me to follow.

Eventually, I had no alternative but to make the decision that I was not going to make this job in Wendover and I called my boss to inform him – this did not go down well.

"The tracker on your van says that you are South of Cheltenham – that's not on the way to Wendover," he snorted.

"My tracker should also show the roads I have driven down to try to find a way out of Swindon, if you care to look," I snapped in response.

"I don't know where I am, all I can see is snow and cars that are stuck on embankments – I am heading home," I explained.

"You are not going home; you are going to Wendover," shouted my boss.

"And what about my well-being, as you mentioned earlier in the day?" I asked.

"Stuff your well-being – company comes first," he shouted.

"Stuff you and your company and stick your job up your ass – I QUIT!" I replied angrily as I headed home.

I now had the task of telling Angie that I had quit my job and I felt that I had let her down. I had taken enough from this company; the attempts of bullying and the total lack of disregard of HSE rules within this industry was appalling and I was pleased to have quit but what would Angie think? Angie was so understanding and so happy that I had got myself away from such a company.

"Perhaps I will get my old Glyn back now?" she said. "You were becoming a right grumpy git."

She laughed as she tried to cheer me up.

But it was a sign of what the asbestos industry was becoming; a lot of 'new' asbestos surveying companies were springing up and set up by 'old' asbestos surveying bosses – some these bosses had gone into liquidation so many times and were yet setting up other asbestos surveying companies.

In my bid to look for another job, I checked Companies House for registered asbestos surveying companies and I was shocked to see at least five men who had over thirty different companies between them, with most going into liquidation.

The trend seemed to be set up an asbestos surveying company, employ trainees or inexperienced staff, pay them a low wage based on their inexperience, bid for a housing contract charging a low fee, take the money and run.

To be honest, the boss of the company that I had just quit was renting a huge house because if he went into liquidation, the creditors could not take away his home – he didn't own it! Is that a way that a legitimate businessman thinks?

I don't think so.

Nevertheless, I went to bed that evening with a lot on my mind and falling to sleep was to be a huge challenge, but eventually, I nodded off.

Chapter Two

Benjamin Allen 200 Km

2nd of February 2019

Saturday morning soon came around and I woke to the sound of my alarm clock and I didn't dare for one minute contemplate hitting the snooze button, but instead, I jumped straight out of bed and got myself ready for the day ahead.

I was soon packing my bike into the back of my car; Angie was getting ready for work and I was frantically too-ing and fro-ing in and out of the house with a slice of toast in my mouth and taking the occasional sip of tea. All night long, I had been thinking about the day before and the feeling of being out of work; I was quietly packing my cycling gear into the car – my helmet, gloves and drinks bottles, with my mind on work and what job offer I would get next – if I were to get any offers, that is.

Before long, I was driving to Tewkesbury and the start of the Benjamin Allen 200 km, my first qualifying event for the PBP.

The drive along the M5 was better than it was during the week days with less traffic and so the drive seemed faster than usual, but still, I had work issues in my mind and I was replaying the situation over and over in my head.

I got to a car park just off Tewkesbury high street and realised that I had no change for the parking meter and so I called the automated phone number that was displayed at the car park to try to pay for parking.

"Do you want to park vehicle registration ending in GMZ?" called the robotic voice from my phone (which was on loudspeaker).

"NO," I called out loudly.

"Do you want to park vehicle registration ending in PLC?"

"NO," I called out!

This went on for a while as it went through all the company vans that I had registered on the system before I was offered the chance to put my new car registration on to the system and as I was trying to shout my new registration to the phone, I was unaware that a group of market traders on the car park opposite were laughing at what they were seeing.

"Is your new registration ending in HTP?" called the automated voice.

"NO!" I shouted and I shouted my registration at the phone again.

"Is your registration ending in XPP?"

"NO...NO...NO!" I shouted as I realised that the time for the start of the ride was getting close. On that, a market trader came over and changed a five-pound note for five-pound coins and after eventually paying for parking, I started to unload my bike and gear from the back of my car.

"NO...NO...NO!" I shouted as I realised that I had left my cycling shoes at home, these shoes had cleats on the soles to clip onto my pedals, but luckily, I had dual pedals – flat on one side and clips on the other, so I was able to ride with my normal shoes on.

I quickly cycled to the Royal Hop pole pub that was to be the start of this event and I could only assume that the landlord had opened up so early in the morning so us long distance cyclists would have a base to start from and finish at.

I had the route uploaded to my Garmin GPS unit and with that, I would have a detailed turn by turn navigation of the whole route, but I also printed off a document supplied by the organiser should anything happen to my Garmin on the ride.

As a group of cyclists waited at the start line, I couldn't help but notice the huge amount of participants at this event – this may be due to the fact that it was a PBP qualifier and proved how huge the Paris–Brest–Paris event was for Audax cyclists.

As we set off, I just couldn't get into my pace due to the cold weather; it was reported as being minus two degrees and at 7:30 in the morning, it felt a lot colder cycling from the Royal Hop pole pub in Tewkesbury to the first checkpoint at Leominster; we had a beautiful route that took us through Ledbury. I just cycled along at a steady pace and was taking in the views as I rode along with other cyclists passing me along the way, thinking of my work situation as I rode. I was becoming unaware of the time and the fact that there were time limits along the route of this event and it wasn't until I stopped to take a bite of a snack that I realised I had about an hour to reach the first checkpoint, which was now eight and a half miles away.

Taking a long sip of my drink, I jumped back on the bike and rode like mad, the cold breeze on my face was feeling like an arctic blast of wind and my ears were numb with cold.

Thankfully, the first checkpoint was not as far away as I first thought and I reached the point with half an hour to spare. I got my Brevet card stamped (proof of passage through each checkpoint) and carried on without stopping for a drink or snack for I wanted to make up the time in the early stages of the ride – in case anything untoward were to happen in the later stages of the day.

I was now on my way to Hay on Wye, which was 36 km away from the first checkpoint and with my mind focused on the time limits, I pushed on with such effort that the road to the next checkpoint was soon with me and at a cafe called 'The Sandwich Cellar'.

I was still mindful of the time and just as keen to make up as much time as I could, but fatigue was setting in badly and I needed more than an energy bar and a self-mixed energy drink – so I jumped at the chance to order a bacon sandwich and a pot of tea and gulped them down quickly; this was followed by a can of Coca Cola in a bid to put some much-needed caffeine in my body for the journey ahead.

After calculating my time and the fact that I was at the 93.4-km stage of the ride, I realised that another 63 km was between the 'Sandwich Cellar' and the next checkpoint at Hopewell colliery (converting 63 km into 39.1 miles made the distance seem more inviting) and off I rode, with new enthusiasm and for once I had put the thoughts of work out of my mind and was able to focus more on the ride.

The B4348 through Dorstone and Peterchurch seemed to be a very fast road and I was cycling at speeds of 28 to 29 miles an hour with very little effort; this road seemed to go on forever and I was totally amazed at the distance I was covering in such a short time, but after Llanwarne, the hill climbs were to return and sometimes on roads that were just wide enough for a car, snow was still visible due to the sheltered parts of the lane as the trees had blocked the sun, small puddles were still iced over too.

I cycled down a road and noticed a church ruin on my right, and on that I was directed up a small lane and a huge climb uphill that seemed to go on for ages.

Snow and ice were still visible and forced me to cycle a little slower than expected, my Garmin GPS was still my point of navigation and there was no need to use the route sheets that I had printed off.

After cycling over a beautiful bridge toward Coleford, I was met with another lung busting hill climb toward Goodrich and following the B4234, Upper Lydbrook and Lydney were the road signs to follow until I saw a sign that read 'HOPEWELL COLLIERY – TURN RIGHT' and turn right I did, up another gruelling hill! After a hard slog, I was turning into the carpark of the colliery and the next checkpoint at the cafe. The staff had kept the cafe open late to cater to our needs and as I entered the cafe, two other cyclists who were about to leave told me that I was the last cyclist, but I was over an hour and a half within the time limit and another group of cyclists were a few minutes ahead of me, so my performance was good at the moment and I had no need to worry. This meant I could stop for another pot of tea and a huge slice of cake.

I left the colliery cycling down the road that I had just cycled up and rolling downhill fast was great until I was met with a long, sharp uphill climb.

By now, it was dark and the darkness dropped quickly and so my bike lights were turned on which illuminated the road ahead; the temperature had dropped too and the bitter cold was hitting my face as a breeze blew towards me for many miles.

The route ahead was dark as the roads had no lamp posts and even the moon offered no light. Sensing that I was going to reach the finish in great time, I was pushing on even harder to get back as soon as I could, cycling from Coleford to Cinderford via the Forest of Dean was a little daunting as the only light I had to assist me was that on my bike and trying to see beyond the beam was impossible.

Despite feeling a little fatigued, I was flying along the road at great speed until suddenly, everything went dark – pitch black, to be precise and I couldn't even see my hands in front of me.

The battery pack to my lights was drained of power and I quickly used my phone to light up the inside of my saddle bag and started to search for my spare light and battery pack, but to my horror, I had left them behind with my cycling shoes.

I just stood there in a stunned state of mind and thinking what the hell do I do now? It was too dark to walk along these roads, let alone cycle without lights. I just stood there for what seemed ages with a heavy heart; I was contemplating the fact that I would be stuck in the middle of nowhere with no plan of what to do next.

Using my phone to offer me some light was the only sensible thing to do; I could be a little more visible to traffic while I stood there and try to think of a solution to my problem, but with cars tooting their horns at me as a way to tell me to keep out of the way even though I was off the road and on a grassy bank (I think), there wasn't much more I could do.

It wasn't long before a concerned driver stopped alongside me to ask if I was okay and after explaining the situation, he gave me a cheap torch he had in his car.

"Take this mate, it will keep you safe until you reach Tewkesbury – which is eight miles away mate," he said as he handed me the torch.

I thanked him and cycled on nervously as I was trying to balance the torch beneath my right hand and the handlebar of my bike; the light was dim but just enough to light a safe road for me to cycle at a decent speed until the battery pack to my Garmin had died and along with it my GPS. This was due to me using the battery pack to power my Garmin Virb video camera and GPS without checking that it was fully charged in the first place.

Again, I searched my bag for the spare battery pack to my Garmin but I had left it at home. I had also left behind the printed route description of the event!

"What do I do now?" I shouted out loud. "How do I navigate my way back?"

"Think Glyn, think…think…think…" I kept saying to myself until an idea hit me. The organiser of this event had emailed links to download onto my Garmin and with it a word document description of the route which had road by road, turn by turn details of the route (which I printed but left at home). I was able to access this on my phone and by stopping every half mile, I was navigating my way to the finish. I was becoming aware of the time and praying for a miracle to happen to help me out of this situation, God must've heard my prayer because soon afterwards, a car was driving behind me and frantically flashing its headlights.

I stopped and turned around to see what was happening – it was the man who gave me the torch and as he stepped out of his car, he shouted, "Hey mate – I cannot allow you to cycle along these roads in the dark with that pathetic torch, what if I drive behind you with my headlights on full beam to light your way?"

I was choked and just managed to shout, "Yes please, if you don't mind."

My eyes were filling with tears to the fact that I was going to make it back to Tewkesbury and safely too.

Those last six miles were done at around twelve miles an hour, the whole road was lit up and my vision was as far as I would want to see, the car behind would be giving me protection from any vehicle that may be coming from behind and I was wiping away the tears as I rode along – tears of joy in the knowledge that I was safe and all thanks to this hero who came to my rescue.

The country lanes were narrow and would have been too dangerous to cycle along in the pitch darkness of the night, but I had a Samaritan driving behind me and lighting the way ahead.

As we reached the illuminated streets of Tewkesbury, the driver slowly overtook me and wound down his window to shout out, "GOOD LUCK MATE!" as he waved to me.

"Thanks mate, thanks," I shouted back.

He drove off in the distance and yet I didn't get to know his name. *What a star, what a hero,* I thought to myself as I

31

cycled to the Royal Hop pole hotel car park and the finish of this qualifier.

I got my Brevet card stamped and after examining the time entries and stamps on the card, the organiser gave me a thumbs up and shouted, "Well done, Glyn." A sign that my first qualifier for the PBP was done.

On this, other cyclists gave me a pat on the back and congratulated me – I was so delighted, I wanted this so badly and yet I thought that I had thrown it all away by not checking my gear before leaving home and by the skin of my teeth, I did it… I did it.

I returned to my car and packed my bike away, jumping in the driver's seat I called my wife on my handsfree and tearfully, I shouted, "Sweetheart, I did it and I am on my way home."

"Drive safely," Angie replied.

I drove back along the M5 and stopped at Strensham services for a cup of tea and a bite to eat, still in my cycling gear with speckles of dirt up the back of my jacket (which is why I got funny looks as I ate my chicken nuggets and drank my tea).

The events of the previous day had certainly put me in a wrong state of mind and to even get to the start line was an achievement, but to take on the 126-mile distance and all that fate threw at me – and survive was perhaps a sign that this year I would be taking on the Paris–Brest–Paris and succeed (we'd see).

I woke up Sunday morning to an empty house; it was Angie's rota to work on Sunday and she left me a cup of tea before she went to work.

I just curled up in bed, all wrapped up under the duvet – nice and warm.

I was feeling the effects of the previous day's ride, my legs were aching and my head was spinning as if I was coming down with a heavy cold.

Oh well – I won't have the hassle of calling in sick at work, I thought to myself.

I wearily got out of bed at around 11 am and steadily walked downstairs (gripping the handrail as if my life depended on it) and I sat on the settee with a mug of tea and watching TV, I nodded off only to wake up at half past two in the afternoon and though I was still tired, I made my way upstairs and jumped in the shower. I was wishing we had a bath in the house so I could soak my tired legs and the inflatable hot tub that I bought in the summer would take too much time and effort to put up now – oh well, the shower would have to do.

After getting dressed, I was ready for something to eat but too lazy to cook anything and so the microwave came into play, a ready meal and a cup of tea had put me in a better mood and I felt my energy coming back to me as the day went on.

The day was spent watching football and searching for jobs on the internet and the prospect of me finding work within my industry was looking bleak, I would admit, but God bless LinkedIn. I got notifications of who was looking at my profile and this was followed by making contact with these folks and their companies in the hope that something would come my way – but I wasn't holding out much hope.

Angie came home from work later in the afternoon and though she tried to be her usual cheery self, she could sense the burden of worry that I was feeling.

She talked of her day at work and I told her of the previous day's ride by giving her a mile-by-mile account of the day with the highs and lows included.

"You will make Paris, I know you will," she said through her ever-beaming smile.

"I hope so, I really hope so," I sighed in reply.

"But you know, if a job comes along that interferes with my training – then Paris will have to be cancelled," I continued.

"Bills come first?" she asked.

"Every time, cycling doesn't pay the bills, unfortunately," I sighed again.

The week that followed should have been seven days of hitting the road on my bike but I had to look for work – I needed to get my name out there and to the right folk.

It seemed that my efforts were paying off as three different companies were phoning me to conduct interviews over the phone in a matter of two days, one company was based in Yorkshire and wanted an asbestos surveyor who was prepared to work away in London every week with the odd week working away in Scotland.

I didn't want to accept this offer but if it was the only job to be offered, then I would have to accept it. Another was a London-based company which wanted an asbestos surveyor to work away each week in Yorkshire – yes, confusing, I agree, but in both cases, I didn't want to live in a hotel room Monday to Friday and just see Angie at weekends (especially as she worked some Saturdays too).

My third telephone interview was giving me some real hope as a long chat was showing positive signs of me finding something local and something that would work round my training and so a 'face to face' interview was arranged for the following Friday at an office in Bristol (though this company was so far away, they had an office in the West Midlands too, which was something that would suit me).

The drive to Bristol was a little tedious as the rain had now turned into a torrential downpour and the M5 was like a river in places, I turned up the radio in a bid to drown out the rattling noise made by the rain hitting my car.

The windscreen wipers were swishing at full speed but making very little difference to the bombardment of rain bouncing from my screen, needless to say that the drive was a lot slower than expected and I arrived a little late for my interview – fortunately, so did the guy who was to interview me.

The interview went well and I felt positive about how I had presented myself, I knew my stuff and I knew how professional I was in my work and I projected that well in the interview – I would just have to wait and see.

The drive back home was really bad with a car accident on the M4; there was a long queue of traffic at a standstill and so I drove in the opposite direction along the M4 to Swindon and a route home that I knew only too well. This put an extra hour on my journey but it was better than sitting on a motorway for God knows how long.

Eventually, I reached a stretch of road that I was so familiar with – the A419, for I had driven along this stretch of road many times in my previous employment and as usual, I took the usual detour through Birdlip to avoid the long queue of traffic that stemmed from the roundabout ahead.

I got home a little before 5 pm and yes it had been a long day but hopefully a day that would be rewarding for me and see me back in work.

Saturday was little better for the rain had stopped but the roads were wet and slippery but this 'man on a mission' needed to get on his wheels and add some much-needed miles to his training.

And off I went in a 'make it up as you go along' attitude – this meant I had no particular place in mind and I would cycle, outward bound, for around twenty miles before starting to cycle back home. This attitude was to show my state of mind at the present time because trying to qualify for the Paris–Brest–Paris was no longer my priority, getting a job was the most important task for me at the moment – no job, no wages would result in not being able to afford to go to Paris anyway and so the training would be totally pointless, but I had to maintain my training in the belief that I would gain employment and my circumstances would change for the better and therefore PBP would be possible.

Yes, it sounds confusing but that was the state of mind I was in at the time as work was getting in the way of my training, but without work, I wouldn't be able to travel to the qualifiers and (hopefully) the PBP in August, and so I needed to find a balance between the two.

My absence from any kind of work would see me going to my local cycle centre in Longbridge, Birmingham and talk to the one man who knew how to keep me motivated – Clint. Clint set up his shop '3CJ' cycle Centre a few years previously and set me up on a bike that was ideal for me – a bike that allowed extra 'leg room' to accommodate my titanium replacement right knee (I have minimal bend in my right knee and need a different bike frame to one that would suit my height).

Now, why a cycle shop would be named '3CJ' had puzzled me and it wasn't long before I asked the question. The answer was that in Clint's family, there were three members whose names began with the letter 'C' and one family member whose name began with the letter 'J' and so the name reflected a family run business and more so, any customer was treated like an extension of the family, which is why I spent most days eating slices of cake and drinking cups of tea while chatting to Clint.

"Don't give up on your dream, mate," Clint replied to me as I was telling him of my woes.

"You need a change of jobs and with your experience of being a community dodgeball coach, a father of a special needs son and your list of sporting achievements – you need to be in a job that sees you coaching and inspiring others into fitness," Clint added.

And when I returned home later in the day, I set about looking on the internet for any roles in that area and so my confidence in finding work was high and I was feeling more relaxed.

The Tuesday that followed my interview was to see me celebrate some good news as I received a phone call.

"Good morning, Glyn. How are you?" came this woman's voice.

"Errm, I am okay I guess – who are you, if you don't mind me asking?"

"I am the person who has been given the task of saying congratulations, we want to offer you a position in our company," she added.

"YESSS…oh… YESSS!" I shouted out.

"I take it you accept then," she laughed.

"Yes, I accept – when do I start?" I asked with a huge grin across my face.

"Can you start Monday?" she asked.

"Yes, see you on Monday," I replied.

I couldn't wait to call Angie and give her the good news, but Angie was a little apprehensive and told me not to accept a job just because I felt that I needed to accept it.

"I have already accepted it," I told her, "and it can't be any worse than the bullying company I had worked for previously."

And so, I was in a positive frame of mind; a new job and a new attitude – I felt that every time I got knocked down I would always bounce back and yes, I had bounced back and life felt great again. The change in my working career had been so unexpected as I never thought I would have a new change of jobs and yet I had worked for three different companies in such a short time.

Feeling more confident, I decided to book a hotel near the start-line at the Velodrome in Saint-Quentin-en-yvelines because the hotels near the start-line became fully booked so early in the year, but how surprised was I when I booked a hotel room so easily?

I was later to discover that the start-line was at a different venue and in fact at Mortagne, some 20 miles from the Velodrome, and booking another hotel near the start/finish-line was a little more difficult but I managed to book somewhere close to the venue and with Angie wanting to come along, I was now looking forward to the training ahead.

My one concern was that Angie would be on her own in France for over three days while I took on the route and so Angie registered as a volunteer/marshall on the event as not to be alone while I cycled; this had now become a more exciting event for us both.

Chapter Three

The Ride from Hell

I started my new job with some enthusiasm but part of me was still worried about how this job would end – when I first started out as an asbestos surveyor some twelve years previously, companies were great to work for as there were not many asbestos surveyors around at the time.

Fast forward to the present day and new companies were springing up everywhere and bidding for contracts for a stupid amount in a bid to undercut other companies.

Charging far too less than they should for a contract meant that setting on experienced surveyors like myself would not be cost-efficient and these companies were setting on 'trainees' and rushing them through their 'P.402' (asbestos surveying competency qualification).

These beginners would be conducting surveys in a totally amateur attitude and if they made mistakes – then they would be sacked and their job taken over by another 'trainee'.

The term 'pay peanuts and you get monkeys' was (and still is, as far as I know) what some asbestos surveying companies were adhering to as profit far outweighed the importance of producing true competent asbestos surveys for their clients and as I was aware, these 'sacked' newly qualified asbestos surveyors were now jumping from company to company and working for a wage that was far little than experienced asbestos surveyors like myself got paid.

With that in mind, I was so pleased to find a job with a reputable company who was willing to pay me my worth and in return I would give them work worthy of my salary.

With the distraction of being unemployed out of the way, I was now able to concentrate on my task, the PBP and the qualifiers ahead with the next one being a 300-km on Saturday, the 16th of March.

With my new job seeing me work in Newbury Berkshire, Abingdon and surrounding areas of Oxfordshire – I was yet again struggling to get home to put in the training I needed to get through my next qualifier. And so, I would get home and get changed into my cycling gear and jump on my Tour de France 5.0 exercise bike, this bike was made by Proform and was powered by Google Maps.

I would have pre-prepared routes mapped out on my I-fit account and I could cycle anywhere in the world from the luxury of my home but this bike would follow every contour of the roads on the route, it was the most realistic exercise bike you could get (and was used by some Tour de France cyclist, as I was told). The weekend of the 300-km was upon me and I was feeling up for the challenge despite the weather being appalling and the forecast saying that the weather was to take a turn for the worse over the weekend.

The start was from a village just outside of Tewksbury and started at six o'clock in the morning. We were barely into the first mile of the ride when the rain started to fall and was to get heavier over the period of the event.

I had set off with a group of cyclists and the chat made the miles pass quickly, but the weather was getting worse with the rain becoming torrential and the light winds was now gale force (and this was before we reached the mountains in Wales where the weather would definitely be worse).

I reached the first checkpoint in good time and with a number of cyclists ahead of me but quite a few behind me too, which told me that I was maintaining my good pace.

The route would have been an amazing journey of great views and scenery but with the gale blowing rain in my face and feeling like someone was throwing grit at me, I could barely see the surrounding scenery but kept my eyes on the road ahead of me.

Reaching Talybont on Usk was the most gruelling part of any challenge that I had taken on, if the gale force winds and torrential rain wasn't bad enough – the hill climbs made everything ten times worse. All along this ride, I was thinking to myself that if the wind was against me on the ride out, it would be behind me on the way back and may make the ride a little easier on the journey to the finish (how wrong was I as I realised that the wind and rain was to be against me all the way from start to finish).

At the Talybont checkpoint, I realised that I had lost thirty minutes on my pace and needed to make that up, so I got my Brevet card stamped and jumped straight back on my bike.

The road was wet, slippery and flooded in parts – my clothes were soaked (even my water proof clothes, proving that they weren't torrential rain proof).

I reached Abervagenny and had a 'cup of tea stop' at a petrol station/cafe/supermarket kind of place. It must have been at this stop where the cyclists I had left behind at the Talybont checkpoint had passed me without me realising.

I got back on my bike (a little delicately, I may add) and set off in the dark evening and this time with my lights switched on and my spare lights in my bag (unlike the 200-km ride).

It wasn't long before I found myself on the B4325 which was the road to Chepstow, but on this road was a long, long hill climb which must have been three of four miles of continuous climbing before reaching the top of the summit – on this road, three other cyclists passed me who shouted, "Keep going mate, you're doing well," as they rode past.

I was about two thirds up this hill (or bloody mountain as it seemed) when I decided that I needed an excuse to get off the bike for a couple of minutes to catch my breath and so I used the excuse of needing a wee for the reason to stop.

As I stood behind a tree and started to relieve myself, I looked at the view from where I was stood, the street lights in the distance below looked like little burning embers on a fire and signalled the houses that were in the distance – it also signalled how high I was up this 'bloody' hill and I still had more hill to climb before reaching the top.

I made it to the top and enjoyed a fast roll down the hill with the chance to rest my legs after the constant uphill pedalling but the roads were wet, slippery and the only light I got was from my bike light and sometimes the moonlight – so applying a little more brakes came into play.

Actually, I had over-used my brakes on this ride as downhill cycling became a hazard with the head wind and partially flooded roads.

Eventually, I reached the Clifton suspension bridge and horror of all horrors, a temporary road sign read:

'LEFT-HAND SIDE OF BRIDGE CLOSED, PEDESTRIANS PLEASE CROSS OVER TO THE OTHER SIDE USING UNDERPASS!'

"WHAT THE HELL?" I screamed to myself. I needed to be on the left side of the bridge so I could get to the next checkpoint at Slim bridge.

I followed the diversion and cycled up and down a path before deciding to cross a footbridge to the other side of the suspension bridge, reaching a petrol station, I stopped to ask for directions to Thornbury and then Slimbridge.

How shocked was I when I was told that a group of cyclists were ahead of me and had passed about half an hour previously? This prompted me to check my time and gave me the sad realisation that I was at risk of being timed out at the next checkpoint.

I hit that road like a bat out of hell and despite the relentless fall of rain, the dark lanes ahead and the light wind that had died down from a gale, I was on a mission to reach the checkpoint within the time limit (even though I knew that this would be difficult at the moment).

I raced down unlit lanes and stopped briefly to check my route sheet as I was losing faith in my GPS unit for some unexplained reason. I was cycling up and down the same lane as I realised that I missed a left turn at one junction of the lane. Eventually, I was able to gather my bearings in a dark and unlit road and I reached Slimbridge in a wet, tired and pathetic state but only to find the checkpoint closed!

What was I to do now? I took a photograph of the checkpoint that was a cafe called the 'Bike Shed' to prove that

I had cycled the correct route (even though my Garmin GPS was proof enough).

All I could do was carry on back to Tewkesbury and to the finish where my car was parked and so I carried on following my GPS unit that was now having difficulty recognising the dirt paths along the river.

By now, it was well after midnight and I was thinking of looking for a hotel to sleep for the night as the thought of a hot shower was becoming more and more welcoming, but I cycled on and followed my GPS unit on to a canal towpath and eventually to Gloucester.

It was in Gloucester city centre that my GPS unit had a dizzy fit and in the city's canal basin (an area of shops and cafes – all closed at a time that I needed a hot drink) with my GPS appearing to send me in all directions – which way do I exit this area?

In all directions I could see concrete stairs, surely, I shouldn't have to carry my bike up those?

Not long afterwards, a group of people came to my help and informed me that a group of cyclists were in the near distance and had passed through a little ahead of me – this gave me new strength and though I knew that because I had not had my card stamped at Slimbridge, I was deemed out of the event – I was now on a mission to prove to myself that I would have done this ride had it not been for the weather conditions.

As I rode out of the city, I saw a sign in the distance that read, 'TEWKESBURY 10 MILES'.

"YES… YES… COME ON, NEARLY THERE!" I shouted to the darkened sky as the rain got heavy again and the winds were now gale force again.

I cycled as if my life depended on it and counted each mile as I rode, the dark and unlit country lanes that weaved left and right; the hills were tough but I took them on as a personal challenge and it was personal, personal between me, the route, the terrain and the bloody weather – I was not going to be beaten! I reached the finish a little more than thirty minutes out of the time limit and with a stamp missing from my card – I could not claim this ride for the PBP as a qualifier but I claimed is as a personal achievement and was a little less disappointed than I should have been.

I was to learn that some had quit the ride because of the weather conditions and had booked into Bed and Breakfast establishments to rest before heading home the following day – so the whole weekend was a tough challenge for everyone.

Feeling sore from the weekend ride, I was aware that another ride was to be taken on during the weekend that followed – 24th of March (eight days after the 300 km) I was entered on the 66-mile 'MAD MARCH HARE' event that started and finished at Longbridge, Birmingham.

The Sunday morning was pleasant with the weather being kind (sunny but not too hot), I set off in a 'conservative' pace and was focused on finishing in a good time but not a record-breaking time.

My legs were still heavy from the previous weekend and it took a few miles to get my legs to accept that we were at it again – cycling for a long distance.

Just like the previous weekend, the scenery was stunning with views that had me stopping from time to time to take photographs – this was not a qualifier for any event and so I rode with a great pace but a speed that was comfortable and manageable from start to finish.

The route had taken us through some beautiful countryside and toward Stourport on Severn before heading back to Longbridge through Worcestershire.

I finished in a time of six hours and thirty-one minutes which was okay, I guess, but I was only bothered about beating the eight-hour time limit because two failures in two consecutive weekends would not have been acceptable to myself.

After the 'Mad March Hare' ride, I was at home and on the internet looking for a 300-km qualifier to take on as a qualifier for the PBP and hopefully success would be on the cards next time.

Work was becoming tedious as the distance that I was driving would be over two-hundred miles a day – everyday!

I had entered another 300-km PBP qualifier but decided to withdraw as I felt that the long hours at work hadn't given me enough time to do the training I needed and so I just wasn't confident enough to take on the challenge at that particular time but I needed to qualify on a 300-km event.

With the time limit closing in on the 300-km qualifier, I entered the 'Green and Yellow Fields' 300 km which would be on the May bank holiday weekend and would give me a little more time to boost my training. The 'Green and Yellow Fields' event started and finished at Manningtree train station and went from Sussex through Suffolk and Norfolk before heading back to Sussex.

With this being my final 300-km chance to qualify for the PARIS–BREST–PARIS I was adamant that I would be prepared for anything and everything that the weather could throw at me and preparing myself for cycling through the dark hours was also needed.

After a day that would see me drive to work at six o'clock in the morning and getting home after 6 o'clock in the evening, I would jump on my bike and do a 'go with the flow' type of attitude to my training in the darkened evening hours – I was tired after a long, hard day's work but this kind of approach to my training could actually benefit my cycling on the day of the event; maybe help me to be mentally fit enough to push through moments of fatigue.

I was now enjoying my training even though my attempts to ride the distances I needed in training was thwarted by work, driving to London and back for three days in a row was a huge upset to my routine – leaving home at 5 am and not getting home until 7 pm rendered me too tired to train and I was now thinking that I should be thinking that the PBP was not going to happen for me even though I wasn't going to quit easily.

A problem was now beginning to show in the form of twinges to my lower back that eventually turned into full out back pain, my GP diagnosed muscular strain bought on by my job and the long distances I was driving was only adding to my problem.

I was prescribed painkillers but I was reluctant to take them and only used them when my pain became unbearable, was I ever going to qualify for the PBP?

After each day's work, I would sit at home and get my wife to rub some kind of pain relief onto my back.

Angie was doing her best to keep me motivated and to keep me in a confident frame of mind.

"I know you too well, Glyn," she said to me. "No matter what – you will dig in deep and do your next qualifier, you will do it."

If only I had her confidence, my back was causing me some real pain but I hid this pain from Angie as best I could because she was a genuine carer and would worry a lot for me – so a smile was my way of hiding my pain.

At my local cycle shop (3CJ Cycle centre, Longbridge) I was lucky to have at my request some great knowledge and advice from Clint, the shop owner.

It was Clint who helped my progress further in cycling by helping to choose the correct bike for my build and with little adjustments, I had a bike that felt like it was custom built for me.

My Cube attain disc pro was like riding on a cushion of air with minimal vibration as I cycled along roads, I was able to ride further and more comfortable than ever and if I were to successfully qualify for the PBP – it would be on my Cube bike.

At 3CJ, Clint was discussing my better options for qualifying for Paris–Brest–Paris and he was advising using a tubeless tyre on the rear of my bike (but not the front wheel) as this would benefit me in the way of not having to waste time fixing any punctures on my next event (should I get a puncture). The idea was that because a tubeless tyre was glued to the rim of a wheel and then filled with a slime substance, if any puncture were to appear in the tyre, then the slime would fill the hole and I could carry on riding without having to stop and fiddle about with taking my wheel off, perhaps I would have to pump my tyre up a little but that would be it – also a kit that contained grommets that you put into the tyre should you have a bigger puncture was an option too, and one I should have been considering.

But before I was to consider any other options, I had to decide if I was fit enough to take on another qualifier as my back was still causing me some grief.

In the run up to the 300 km on the May Day bank holiday, I was now in two minds as to take part or just forget about taking on the challenge, my back was aching and my training had dropped due to long hours at work.

I sat down with Angie and asked her to offer some advice, I guess I needed a reason to either quit, on someone else's recommendation (I couldn't feel guilty if my wife advised to quit), or just go for it and hope for the best.

Angie's advice was, "You completed a 300-km ride a month ago and despite the appalling weather conditions – you completed the distance, okay, you were out of time because of the conditions, but you battled on and reached the finish…because you have this do or die attitude to everything you do – so bloody go for it."

And there it was, what could I say after she told me that – other than, "BRING IT ON!"

Chapter Four

Green and Yellow Fields

I was now working for a company who seemed to appreciate its staff and the attitude shown towards me was great from the company; each day was a relaxed kind of feeling but because of the long hours of driving, I was enjoying my job a little less.

I had now decided to take on the next qualifier for the PBP and that being the 'Green and Yellow Fields' it seemed that all Audax events had original names to them which made the rides feel more fun (if cycling 190 miles could be fun).

I woke for work on the morning of Friday, the third of May and packed my van with my cycling gear alongside my work tools and yes I had a whole day of work ahead of me before a 190-mile bike which started at midnight (well one-minute past midnight, to be exact).

My good friend Mark (whom I worked with at a previous employment) phoned me to ask how I was and if I would be cycling the weekend.

"You know that it will be a difficult task to work all day Friday and then cycle all day Saturday?" he asked. "You will have almost forty hours with no sleep, do you think that is wise mate?"

"It's not the best situation, I admit, but this is my only option as this is my last chance to qualify on a 300-km ride," I replied.

Mark wished me luck and made me promise to let him know how I did at the event.

I worked hard on Friday as my plan was to finish as early as possible and then drive to Manningtree, Essex for the start of the ride and as I was working in Reading, I thought that the drive to the event would be an hour or so – it was (according to my sat-nav) two and a half hours away.

As I drove from Reading, my sat-nav called out, 'Your route is being recalculated due to traffic issues on the M25.'

There had been an accident and a long queue of traffic was building up and so an extra half an hour was to be added to my journey and by now the rain was falling heavily.

As I drove toward Manningtree, I was looking at the weather and recalling the last 300-km event where I got timed out because of the weather conditions and fearing the worse. I was tempted to drive home instead and as my route was now going through Brent cross and the north circular route around London, I was feeling less confident about the weekend ahead.

My original time for my journey was two and a half hours but this had now doubled and instead of getting to Manningtree at 6:30 pm, I was now looking at 9 pm.

I eventually arrived at my parking space (which I had booked in advance) at ten past nine and as I had over two hours before the start of the event, I decided to get my head down and take some sleep and not forget to set an alarm on my phone to wake me at ten thirty.

I nodded off and I felt that I was having a good sleep but I was woken by a knocking on my windscreen and jumping up in shock, I shouted, "WHAT THE FU—OH HELLO!" as I saw a concerned woman standing by my van.

"Are you okay, dear?" she asked.

I got out and explained why I was there and why I was taking a sleep.

"Oh my, I should have let you carry on with your sleep, I do apologise," she replied.

"No problem," I said. "I needed to wake now anyway to get myself and my gear ready for the ride," I explained as I realised that I had been asleep for over an hour anyway.

After getting changed into my cycling gear, I rode to the start of the ride at Manningtree Train Station where a group of cyclists was beginning to gather; we were all chatting away together about the ride ahead and the hopes of qualifying for the PBP until the sounds of loud chattering was broken by the sound of a huge bang – a car had driven on to the station car park and the bike on his roof rack had smashed against the height restriction barrier with the bike being hurled to the ground.

A group went over to help with the situation but I think the guy was unable to compete as his bike was in need of some serious repair, I just stood there and tried to concentrate on the ride ahead of me as I had no real plan of how I was going to tackle the distance ahead of me.

One cyclist (and a seasoned Audaxer) offered some great advice.

"Treat each stage as a separate ride and aim to get to each checkpoint before the cut of time, that's the target and with four checkpoints comes four separate targets," he explained.

And with the first checkpoint being at a 24-hour McDonalds at Barton mills, I should have been looking at reaching there at around half past four which would give me about an hour before the official cut off time and that's when I had my plan to reach each checkpoint within the time limit and try to build up a bigger time margin at each point (an hour early at each checkpoint multiplied by four checkpoints would equal a finishing time of sixteen hours instead of the twenty hours allowed to complete the ride).

"YES," I was rambling to myself by now but this was my way of keeping myself confident.

One-minute past midnight and we were away, a huge group of cyclists riding into the dark lanes from Manningtree toward Dedham and then Stoke-by-Nayland.

This was a great riding experience as I had never started a ride at midnight before and the thought of finishing in daylight was better than the thought of cycling all day and riding in the dark hours when I may feel more tired and be too fatigued to finish.

As the group rode further, the gaps between cyclists became bigger and so smaller groups of cyclists began to form, I was so happy to have some company with me as it was so different from the previous qualifiers where I was cycling alone for most of the ride.

We reached the 75-km checkpoint at Barton Mills at around 4:15 am – within an hour of the cut off time and as we needed a receipt as proof of passage. I decided on a cup of tea and a portion of fries, gulping these down quickly, I was soon back on my bike and heading for the second checkpoint at Burnham Deepdale on the Norfolk coast, but now the temperature had dropped so much that I was actually dithering as I rode along the A1065 towards Brandon.

By now, the darkness was slowly being replaced by the daylight that was trying to break through and I was hoping that my body clock would start all over again and accept that I need to be in a wide awake mode, but this was not the case as my eyeballs started to roll and my eyelids grew heavy (I was now regretting the whole day at work on Friday and wishing I had taken some midday sleep) and as I cycled along the road, I noticed a figure standing by the side on the pavement and waiting to cross the road which made me slow down to allow him to cross – he just stood there doing nothing and so I slowed down even more, to which he stood still!

"HURRY UP AND CROSS THE ROAD THEN!" I called out to this man who showed no emotion and no recognition of my gesture – until I realised that the man was actually a concrete bollard and on that I got off my bike and gulped down a small bottle of 'caffeine shot' which was followed by an energy bar. As I stood there waiting for the caffeine to kick in, Angie called me to ask how I was doing?

"I am okay – doing fine apart from talking to a brick wall or in my case a concrete bollard," I joked.

"Please keep yourself safe, Glyn, and if need be, book into a hotel," begged Angie.

"I will be fine…just fine," I replied.

And after hanging up, I felt the heaviness of my eyes being lifted and my body felt like it was waking up and maybe the caffeine shot was taking effect.

I was back on form and back on my bike, heading toward the coastal town of Burnham Deepdale via Swaffham, Castle Acre, Great Massingham and Docking.

Now, at this point, I thought that Norfolk was flat until I rode up hills that were muscle aching, heart thumping efforts all the way and with a head wind to deal with too.

The ride to Burnham Deepdale was to become a tough effort but the reward would be that on leaving Burnham Deepdale (the halfway point), I would be cycling with the wind behind me for a long way. And so, after riding through some beautiful towns and villages, I eventually reached the halfway point where a Marshall was waiting to stamp my brevet card as proof of passage and after buying a cup of tea at the Deepdale café, I was back on my bike with around an hour within the time limit.

The next section of the event was a further 61 km (around 37 miles to Wymondham) and unlike the first section, there were two checkpoints on this second half of the ride which was to break the cycling down a little.

The ride through Burnham market to Dereham was relatively flat with a few downhills, but for the appearance of hail storms which came from nowhere.

The hail storms brought back my thoughts of the Tewkesbury attempt as this was soon at the forefront of my mind but I still remained confident and I was focused on the roads ahead and I reached Wymondham within a good time.

The fact that I needed a receipt from the Waitrose cafe as proof of passage gave me a good excuse to buy something substantial to eat but as the queue was a little longer than expected, I had to make do with a small bottle of coke (caffeine) and a two-pack of chocolate cream eclairs and after gulping these down, I was soon on my way to the next checkpoint at Needham Market.

By now, my Garmin GPS had navigated me so well around the course and I had no need to look at the route sheets that I had printed off, until a moment where I was cycling through Kenninghall – taking the B1113 towards Botesdale and as I rode up a small hill, my Garmin informed me to make a U-turn and a **'Off course!'** message flashed on my screen.

I turned around to retrace my tracks but again I was advised to make another U-turn, on this, I got my phone out of my pocket to look on Google Maps for my location but this too was having a dizzy spell as the map just kept rotating on my screen – could it be that I had found a GPS black spot?

And so, I got my route sheets out of my pocket to check where I was but on that, a car stopped to ask if I needed help.

The driver reassured me that I was on the right road and I continued my journey with my Garmin eventually telling that I was, in fact, on the right road, the road ahead was to give me some uphills which were now taking effect on my tired legs and by now my enthusiasm had dwindled a lot as I found myself saying, "Never again – never again, stuff the 400 km and stuff the 600 km – I have had enough," I cursed.

I reached Needham Market and within a time of around forty minutes to spare and the news that I wasn't the last rider on the course but in fact there were six others behind me of which two had decided to quit and as this was an event of personal achievement, it was always a confidence boost to be told that you were not the last rider at an event.

Because the second half of the event was broken down into two checkpoints, it made the section seem a little easier than the first half and when leaving the Needham Market checkpoint, I was pleased to be told that the finish line was a little over sixteen miles away.

With two hours left to reach the finish, I analysed the time and planned a steadier ride back with the use of my Garmin – the plan was to keep in a steady but effective pace and in theory I had the time to cycle at eight miles per hour for the last two hours if needed but instead to keep to a comfortable ten miles per hour and finish relaxed.

That last sixteen miles seemed to take forever and I was constantly gazing at my Garmin until I cycled from a narrow country lane and onto a main road with a sign that indicated Manningtree train station was near, on that, I increased the pace and picked up the speed.

I reached the train station in Manningtree with my Garmin indicating a time of 17:30 hours but in real time and adding the stops for tea and food – I finished within a time of 19:30 hours, not a fast time, but I did it within the time limit and that's all that mattered.

I reached my van and slowly packed away my bike and after calling Angie and giving her the good news, I told her that I was done – the PBP was over, I didn't want to do another qualifier ever again – never!

"We will see," replied Angie. "We will see."

The drive home was to take me around two and a half hours which meant I would be home for midnight as the journey would be the A14 and the M6 but as soon as I reached the A14, I felt my eyes getting heavy and was forced to pull into a lay-by for a sleep, I repeated this eight times and eventually got home at 5 am the following morning.

Angie was a little concerned and had woke up to call me at different times throughout the night and she was so relieved to see me home safe and sound.

After a shower and a few hours' sleep, I woke up to a wife who was so eager for me to tell her how I got on, how I felt and to tell her all the highs and lows of the ride – this was what I needed to encourage me to continue with my goal to qualify for the PBP and make me look forward to the 400-km qualifier.

"So, you are still going for it – the PBP is still on?" asked Angie.

"Yeah…on reflection, I worked hard yesterday and now I am halfway to qualifying…so yes, it's still on," I sighed.

Angie, who is a cyclist herself (well, she became a cyclist when she met me and wanted to ride alongside me on training sessions) reminded me that in a week's time, I was taking part in the Birmingham and Midlands Velo – 100 miles of cycling on already tired legs.

"How do you rest but maintain your training for next weekend?" she asked.

"I will just ride easier sessions for a couple of times during the week, I guess," was my reply. "Anyway, if I don't complete it – it's not the end of the world, is it?" I sighed.

Chapter Five

Birmingham and Midlands Velo

I was now on a high as the realisation of qualifying was becoming a reality, I had completed a 200-km and 300-km qualifying event and had just two more events to complete – 400 km and 600 km, which besides physical strength and stamina, needed great mental strength too.

At work, I was back into a routine of long hours and my training had once again dropped, it was becoming clear that with some asbestos surveying companies who had housing contracts, they would demand more work and this was due to the fact of putting in a competitive bid to secure the contract and a smaller fee was charged to the housing association or council for each property – to make the contract profitable, more properties needed to be surveyed each day to make the job pay.

I loved my job but I was one of the most experienced in my profession and had worked on huge commercial and industrial sites and to be on housing contracts was like a step back to me but I looked on the bright side – with tenanted housing, I was always guaranteed a cup of tea.

Almost a week had passed since my 300-km (190-mile) ride and I was soon getting my bike ready for the 100-mile Velo around Birmingham and the Midlands.

Sunday, the twelfth of May, I woke up at 5 am to get ready for a big day, the Velo was huge and with 17,000 competitors signed up; it was to be a great event.

Angie drove me and my bike to Edgbaston Cricket Ground and I cycled to the start line, while steadily riding to Birmingham's Digbeth area, I was going over my plan for the day. If I rode at a steady 12-mph, I would finish within an hour and half of the time limit and my legs would feel better than if I pushed hard and tried to break a personal record. Anyway – it was not a PBP qualifier so I wouldn't lose anything.

The start line was buzzing and as each group of cyclists went off at different times, I waited patiently for my start time of 8 am – my start time seemed to come around quickly and we were off, cycling out of Digbeth and towards Small Heath – along the A45 for a short distance before heading toward Sheldon and Marston green.

It wasn't long before we were cycling toward Coleshill and heading towards Atherstone, I knew these roads very well from when I worked for a company who had a contract with North Warwickshire council and I would take my bike with me to train around these roads and country lanes at the end of most working days – and so it felt like I was cycling around home as I rode along the too familiar roads of the route.

I was now looking at my Garmin GPS and I was happily surprised to see that my average speed was 15.6 mph and even though my legs felt heavy from the previous weekend – I didn't feel that I was putting in too much effort and was really comfortable with my speed.

I was now confident of finishing with a much better time than I expected and with the attitude of using the Velo as a training session for my next PBP qualifier, I was in a much better frame of mind.

All was going well until we were cycling downhill on the Coleshill road near Atherstone when we all came to a sudden stop; a huge crowd of cyclists just standing there for over thirty minutes wondering what had happened.

An ambulance drove its way through the crowd who were making a human pathway for the vehicle to go through to attend to a fellow cyclist who had come off his bike and was in a bad way – so bad that an air ambulance whisked him to hospital.

As we were steadily getting back into our pace and beginning to pick up the speed again, we couldn't ignore a bike propped up against a fence in the usually quiet country lane and a smashed cycling helmet on the road that was surrounded by a huge pool of blood, this was a sign of a much serious accident but with the roads closed off to all traffic – thankfully, the cyclist had not been hit by a passing car and thoughts of a speedy recovery for the cyclist were on everyone's mind.

However, my Garmin GPS was now telling that my average speed was 12.8mph and this was due to the time lost on the Coleshill road – so I was determined to gain the time back and pushed hard on the pedals to put me back on my planned average speed.

I would take time to say that I did respect all fellow cyclists of any speed or ability but sometimes you saw someone who made you think, WHAT THE HELL?

I saw one cyclist who on a few occasions fell off his bike at road junctions and his falls were due to the fact that he couldn't get his shoes unclipped from his pedals – he would just stop at a junction and fall to his left or right in a sitting position on his bike…lying there in the road with his bike on top of him. At one time, I stopped to help him and I asked, "You have practised the use of cleats, clipped shoes and pedals and all that?"

"No," came the reply. "My mate told me that cleats would make me faster and so I changed my pedals yesterday and bought a new pair of cycling shoes with cleats."

After telling him that his decision should have been made weeks ago and given him time to get used to his new pedals, I showed him how to quickly release his feet from his pedals – it seemed that he was trying to pull his legs upwards to release his feet from the pedals when he should have twisted his feet outwards and after demonstrating how I used my cleats, he seemed to be getting the hang of it.

After this situation, my average speed had dropped again and I was seeing my Garmin display telling me that 12.7 mph was now my average speed – I needed to pick up the pace.

I pedalled hard to Coventry which was the forty-two-mile checkpoint of the ride and the finish for those who had signed up for the smaller distance of the event. As I left Coventry, I was cycling along (once again) familiar roads and country lanes toward Solihull and Knowle.

By now, the weather got warmer and sunnier, the crowds had become bigger and the noise louder as folk cheered the cyclists that were riding through their towns and villages and at one-point, members of staff of a care home who had sat their elderly residents on the front lawns shouted out, "THANK YOU FOR MAKING OUR DAY!" in recognition of how their residents were enjoying the event. I slowed down to give the elderly folk a huge wave and thank them for their support on which one elderly woman shouted in jest, "Get a tandem for next year and I will join you!" This was met with a huge wave of laughter from cyclists and the crowds spectating.

It wasn't long before we were to see a huge Birmingham and Midlands official sign that read 'WELCOME BACK TO BIRMINGHAM' and the realisation that the finish wasn't too far away, the route was now on roads that I trained on and a familiar route that would take me within half a mile away from my house – was this a tempting thought to just go home?

It had crossed my mind but I wanted to complete the whole distance and put it down to another huge training session for the PBP qualifiers – and I would get a medal too.

I crossed the finish line in an official time of '7 hours and 48 minutes' and my average speed was 13.1 mph which I was pleased with on the day, however, I was to learn from Angie that the cyclist who was flown to hospital by air ambulance had died – I had phoned my wife to tell her that I had finished and I was making my way home when she gave me the sad news.

A fellow cyclist had died on the event and of course, my heart went out to his family, a 'Just-giving' page was quickly set up in his memory with donations going to the Air ambulance team who tried to save his life – at the time of writing this chapter, over £12,000 had been raised so far in the cyclist's memory.

I jumped on a train at new street station and made my way to Bournville and a three-mile ride home, but that three-mile was really sullen and my mood was so sad and yes I should have been celebrating that I had successfully completed a huge distance on a big local event, but I was heading home to a waiting wife, whereas a fellow cyclist never made it home and that was so heart-breaking.

The next day, I was back at work and with my legs feeling a little discomfort, I was feeling fine and tackled the work easily, news was now coming of idiot car drivers who had been arrested for dangerous driving on the Velo event – one driver who was angry that his road was blocked due to traffic because of safety for the competing cyclists had driven through cones and then mounted the pavement and drove at full speed on the pavement for some distance with total lack of regard for any pedestrians who may have walked out in front of his car!

Another driver just decided to drive through bollards and full on at a Marshall and caused damage to the Marshall's hip, both drivers were arrested with one driver being aged 72 years old – I ask you… Just one Sunday in one year where certain roads are closed off and with residents in the area being notified by post, radio, TV and newspapers about closure to roads – can you accept that drivers claim to be unaware of the event…more importantly, can you understand any driver who would want to risk the safety of cyclists and Marshalls?

Thank God these idiot drivers never caused any other serious safety issues by knocking riders off their bikes and the whole day had gone well with folk lining the streets and setting up unofficial drink stops outside their homes; some villages had a real carnival atmosphere going and steel drums would be playing as we rode past.

But some folks just didn't get into the spirit of the event and the fact that folks from all over the country had travelled to our region to take part – some had booked into hotels and dined at local restaurants, most had gone out shopping the evening before and boosted the local economy; a great reason to have an event like this in our area.

I was to spend the following week working in Stoke on Trent and a relatively easy week of work compared to previous weeks but a tedious drive home each afternoon would get me home later than expected and this was due to the roadworks on the M6 and M5, two busy and congested motorways at the best of times but with roadworks too – I was never getting home too early but I needed some rest anyway from my training and I would pick up my routine towards the weekend.

I was focused on qualifying for the inaugural Paris–Brest–Paris event (PBP) and despite the long hours at work, I was planning my training routine really well. But work had taken a turn for the worse as I was now driving to Warrington, which was taking two and half hours to get there and three hours to get back home, adding the expected eight hours of work made it a long day every day.

I had a 414-km qualifier to take on but training was becoming difficult as my hours were consumed with work, work and more work. The company I was now working for had decided that the honeymoon period was over and they started giving me a work schedule that was almost impossible.

As an asbestos surveyor, you had the great responsibility of ensuring that all asbestos material was accounted for on any site or property, if you missed any materials that contained asbestos and a worker was to drill or smash a panel that contained asbestos and risked breathing in asbestos fibres, then the surveyor would find himself in court if gross negligence seemed to be the reason for missing the item.

Under my work ethics of asbestos being a serious issue and my own personal motto of 'I am making the environment a safer place to work'. I refused to rush through all of my properties just so my company could make an extra couple of quid each day – after all, it would be me in court, not them, if I made blatant errors.

I was now getting home late but jumping on my Tour de France exercise bike to keep my fitness levels up, I would plot a route around New York and plot routes around my home town on my exercise bike would replicate the cycling uphills and downhills too, because I couldn't roll down hills on this bike, I was cycling every inch of the routes that I had set out, making this a harder workout than normal road cycling.

Eventually came the weekend of my 400-km PBP qualifier and the 'Asparagus and Strawberries' 414-km event which started at Manningtree train station and went out to the coastal town of 'Wells-next-the-sea' via Ixworth and Halesworth before heading back through Barton Mills and Saffron Walden.

As before, the nervous anticipation was building up as I realised just how far this ride really was and how long I could ride on my bike for – the other concern was the fact that I had entered only because I failed on a previous 300-km attempt which in turn forced me to cancel a previous 400-km qualifier and reschedule to this event, and though bad weather may have been the reason for failing on that 300-km qualifier, I wasn't guaranteed good weather this weekend either. As was the rule on every Audax ride (regardless of distance), every rider was to be self-sufficient and carried their own food, drink and emergency gear should anything happen to your bike – you also needed to have the means to get home if things went wrong (taxi or train fare).

It was always great to see a steady flow of cyclists set off on an Audax ride, the camaraderie was great and the respect for each other was even greater and so the atmosphere as we set off on this was so relaxed – we were all focused on the first checkpoint at Ixworth which was 50 km or thirty miles away. My game plan was to ride in an economical but effective manner, or put another way – an efficient pace but one that kept me ahead of any time limit at each checkpoint.

This ride was wonderful as I soaked up the wonderful views of the Suffolk countryside and on such a warm morning too, my GPS system was telling that I was cycling at a good pace and one that didn't seem to have me labouring on the uphill stretches either, it was no surprise that I reached Ixworth in good spirits and almost an hour and half ahead of the checkpoint closing time.

I was now on a mission to get to the next checkpoint and hopefully make up even more time, the next checkpoint being Halesworth and as before – I was cycling along country lanes and some stunning views of the Norfolk countryside but what made this stretch of the ride even more welcoming was the Reedham ferry that crossed the River Yare and cost only a pound to get on. This ferry crossing was part of the route and in great Audax style it was what made these rides so memorable – they were always planned to pass towns and villages of interest and beauty and give you a self-guided tour of areas that you may not otherwise see.

Again, I reached Halesworth (107 km or 66.5 miles) in good time and was pleased to see that I was over two hours ahead of the official cut-off time. This was an unmanned checkpoint and a shop receipt was needed as proof of passage which meant that we needed a shop receipt with the date and time on it (and obviously the name of the shop and its address).

The next checkpoint was at Acle which was 107 km or 93 miles and I reached this checkpoint feeling so strong and was now almost three hours ahead of the cut-off time (and boy was I feeling great).

The next checkpoint was at 'Wells-next-the-sea' on the Norfolk coast (218 km or 135.5 miles). Again, the ride was wonderful with stunning scenery along the way. By now, I had accidentally become part of a group who were cycling together and this group were part of the cycling club who had staged this event, so it was great to be allowed to tag along with these riders and benefit from their knowledge of the route – the company made the miles pass by so quickly as we cycled along before reaching the Norfolk coastal town of Wells.

The Wells checkpoint was an unmanned checkpoint which meant that again we needed a shop receipt with the date and time on it. I looked at my brevet card and was so happy to see that I was almost four and a half hours ahead of the cut-off time for this checkpoint – this put an extra spring in my step, I can tell you. This checkpoint was to be closed at 23:32 and here I was at seven o'clock in the evening and taking the mileage at ease but with this great news was to be some bad news, as one cyclist pointed out.

"Did you do a pre-qualifier?" asked the cyclist.

"Pardon?" I asked.

"A pre-qualifier, did you do a pre-qualifier for the PBP last year?" he repeated.

"No – no I didn't," I replied with a surprised expression.

"Well, I am afraid that you can't qualify," he said. "A pre-qualifier is to book your place on the event and then you officially enter the PBP upon completing the four events required."

I was gutted and really deflated, for I had worked so hard to get this far – and not only worked hard but I had overcome issues at work that made my training even more difficult and for what? Nothing, it appeared!

The next part of the ride was to be a long ride to Barton Mills which is a 79-km ride (49.1 miles) through the dark hours of the evening and into the early morning, this section of the ride was taken on with a heavy heart as the thought of not being able to qualify was on my mind. I was eventually able to convince myself that I would find a way of qualifying and that all negative thoughts should be banished from my mind and I needed to remain positive and focused on the event in hand.

And so, after cycling along the A1065 and through Swaffham, I found myself cycling alongside the RAF base in Lakenheath and then onto the McDonalds at Barton Mills which was now the 297-km stage of the ride (or 184.5 miles) and on reaching this checkpoint, I realised that I was three and half hours ahead of the cut-off time. I had lost an hour on the last leg of the ride which could be excused as riding through the dark hours of the evening and cold weather would have slowed me down (but to be honest, the news of the PBP pre-qualifier may have had something to do with it too).

After eating a few fries and chicken nuggets (rinsed down with a cup of tea), I was on my way to the final checkpoint before we reached the finish line and this was to put me back in a positive frame of mind and a pace that I was doing the day before. The country lanes were still very dark and the moonlight was offering some assistance in helping to light the way ahead, of course, we all had very well-lit bikes and our bike lights were of the great standard needed on an event like this. It was the early hours of Sunday morning and as I cycled on I could spot a few cyclists taking a sleep in what is called an 'AUDAX HOTEL' – a bus shelter.

Bus shelters offered great protection from the elements on many Audax rides and as we were having a spot of rain, some entrants took advantage of sheltering at these bus stops. I carried on and just focused on getting to Saffron Waldren which was the 344-km point of the event (213.8 miles) and to ride through the dark hours on any event was somewhat daunting, enthusiasm and pace could drop greatly and in my case – it did. However, I reached Saffron Waldron with three hours to spare which signalled that I had lost thirty minutes in just under forty miles and again the reason for this was the dark lanes, not having full visibility of roads would always put you in a slower and safer pace – but I was still ahead of time and had no possible thoughts of slowing down even more, I was confident of finishing within the time limit.

On my way to Manningtree train station and the finish of this gruelling ride, I was back in a positive frame of mind as the sun was rising and the daylight was breaking through, by now, I was taking off the extra clothing that I had put on to keep me warm through the night. Cycling along in a short sleeve jersey and shorts was so invigorating and my pace had got faster again, but as the day went on, the weather had got hotter and the hills steeper.

I reached the train station at 09:30 and two and half hours within the time limit and another success for my qualification on the PBP.

Chapter Six

Disappointment?

On my way home, I was constantly worrying about the 'pre-qualification' rule for the PBP and so the first thing I did when I got home was to go online and check the rules on the PARIS–BREST–PARIS website and yes, there were rules concerning pre-qualifying events but this was to ensure that you had your name on the entrants list ahead of other cyclists. The complete entrants list would be open to everyone (regardless of any pre-qualifying events) in June.

In a bid to clarify the rules, I emailed the organiser and to my horror the reply I got was, "Dear sir, I am sorry to inform you that this year's event is full and we cannot offer you a place."

I was gutted, totally gutted and with my 600-km qualifying event only a week after my 400-km ride, I pondered on the fact of just simply not bothering to turn up. By this time, I was training with a cycling club near where I lived and that club being Cannon hill cycling club in Birmingham (I was cycling with a club linked to '3CJ' cycling centre in Longbridge too) and so I was really confident about qualifying and the prospect of cycling over

1000 km in the matter of two consecutive weekends wasn't a problem.

The one problem for me would be the fact that my enthusiasm had gone and to give up a whole weekend (600 km or 373 miles in forty hours or less) with the knowledge that I could no longer qualify for the PBP would now be totally pointless, I contacted the organiser of the 600-km to inform him that I won't be making it on the start line – I didn't do the 600-km event.

With the disappointment of the PBP, it was suggested by my wife (as I had booked the next Friday and Monday off work because of the planned 600-km) that we go away for a long weekend instead. We packed our bikes into my van and headed for a friends' caravan in Weymouth.

We set off late Thursday evening and arrived just a few minutes before 11 pm. After having a cup of tea and planning what we were going to do the next day, we went to bed. The following morning, we set off on our bikes and rode along the coastline, even though it was very early morning, it was a warm morning and really enjoyable. It was the first time that Angie had been on her bike for over six months and so the ride was shorter than I had expected, but we did manage eleven miles together and after riding with Angie back to the caravan, I set off again on my own and cycled for a further 26 miles.

Despite cycling along some quaint country lanes and surrounded by stunning views, I was still a little less motivated because of my unplanned withdrawal from the PBP and therefore my pace was to be a little slower than my usual speed. After a weekend of cycling, sightseeing and more cycling – we returned home and back to reality, back to work and the usual routine but without the thought of being stuck on my bike to keep up my training for the PBP. However, less than two weeks after being told in an email that I could not qualify for the PBP, I received an email to inform that due to the high number of entrants who withdrew themselves from the event – I was to be offered a place on the event but only if I had done all four of my qualifiers. I was so angry with myself because if I had done the 600-km as planned, I would now be officially entered on the PBP.

I was given an extension on the time limit to ride a 600-km qualifier but despite this time limit, all the 600-km events were full and I couldn't gain entry into any of them (it may have been the fact that other cyclists in my position had taken advantage of the extension and entered any 600 km they could find). And so, I was facing the disappointment of not making the qualifying events again and decided that I was to have no way of cycling in this year's PBP event – I would have to wait for another four years until the next PBP event.

Work was now becoming tedious and a job I once enjoyed was now a job I was loathing, perhaps I was becoming too old to be an asbestos surveyor – it was a very physical job whereas carrying tools and a ladder across sites before you started work was very hard work, and that was before you started your work – not to mention the two hours' drive to work and the two hours' drive home. I was now blaming my job for my failure to qualify for the PBP and this made me hate my job even more but as I needed my job to pay my bills; I was stuck in a rut. However, I was to receive some good news from Audax UK and Danial Webb, the organiser of the London–Edinburgh–London event (LEL) and this news was that I had qualified and I had a guaranteed place on the LEL 2021 event, the LEL is (like the PBP) staged once every four years and is as prestigious as the Paris event. And so, with two years before I was to ride the LEL, I was back in training mode again.

In between working and training, I managed to find time to join a musical theatre company by the name of 'Arcadians' and on the first day of joining the group, I was (thanks to encouragement from Stella Rourke) in rehearsals for their upcoming production of 'Sweet Charity' and boy did I enjoy this. I was dancing (in a fashion) and I was beginning to try to find a singing voice that I may have. Arcadians musical theatre group helped me regain the confident and happy persona that I have always been known for, I was back to my usual self and I was nervously looking forward to my first performance on stage in front of a live audience.

My life was happy once more and despite issues at work, I was confident enough to brush these aside, and the disappointment with the PBP was now at the back of my mind as I looked forward to other positive things ahead of me – however, I had still booked a week from work and a hotel for the PBP and was hoping to go along to France for a short holiday with Angie until a friend suggested an idea to me. As a huge fan of Queen (and I did cry when Freddie Mercury died in 1991), my friend suggested a bike ride to Montreux, Switzerland and a visit to Freddie Mercury's statue that overlooks Lake Geneva – a great idea and such a great adventure ahead of us if we were to take it on, but as I had only a week from work, the logistics would be a little troublesome.

It was suggested that we tackled it like the Tour De France and take on stages on route to Freddie's statue, but I wanted to ride as much of the route as possible and suggested that I ride from Calais to Switzerland which would be (roughly) 500 miles and if I could cycle 414 km (257.2 miles) in less than thirty hours as I did on the last PBP qualifier that I took part in – I should make the distance in five days or less.

I cancelled my hotel near Paris and booked a camper van for the August week of cycling to Montreux, I booked the journey on the Eurotunnel for the Friday morning (as I managed to book an extra day's holiday from work) and we were all set to go.

Obviously, I spent hours plotting a route and an alternative route should anything go wrong along the way, camp sites and small hotels were included on the route so we had an end of day base to finish at, and with the suggested route of 'Calais–Reims–Chaumont–Luasanne–Montreux' what could go wrong? I was now excited at the thought of visiting the statue of my all-time hero, Freddie Mercury; Queen were all I ever talked about as a teenager – and being a teenager who suffered epilepsy, I was confined to my house and not allowed outside unless I had a chaperone for my own safety. I would spend many evenings in my bedroom listening to my Queen LPs (we didn't have iPods and downloads in 1977, we didn't have the internet or cable TV either).

It was ironic that in 1984, Queen released a song that reached number two in the charts and that song was 'Radio Ga Ga', every time I heard the line, "*I'd sit alone and watch your light, my only friend through teenage nights*," I would shed a tear – for this one line explained my life as a teenager with epilepsy. I would sit alone in my bedroom and have my record player as my only comfort, my only friend through teenage nights.

And so, visiting Freddie's statue in Montreux was to be a huge but rewarding challenge for me to take on. I had met Brian May (Queen's lead guitarist) back in 1994 and I had a photo to prove it but I had never met Freddie Mercury and so this would be as good as meeting the man himself.

My routine was now – training on my bike, rehearsals with Arcadians and work, but not with the feeling of being in a rut and I had a spring in my step once again, this spring in my step was down to the fact that rehearsing for a musical production was the most happy and uplifting experience I had and I was looking forward to rehearsals each week.

Being in a hall and belting out songs such as 'The Rhythm of Life', 'There's got to be something better than this' and 'I always cry at weddings' was so joyful. I was now dancing (in a fashion) and at home, I would rehearse my lines and my songs so much that my wife was now suffering from an aching of the ears as I would go into a rendition of 'I always cry at weddings' and for some reason that song was stuck in my head as I would sing it everywhere I went – in the shower, in my car – everywhere.

The Paris–Brest–Paris (PBP) was scheduled for the week of Saturday, the 18th of August to Thursday, the 22nd of August 2019, but now I was planning to cycle from Calais to Montreux from Friday, the 17th of August and hopefully reach Freddie Mercury's statue by Thursday. The invitation to come along with me was open to Angie but she declined the invitation and suggested a 'lads' week away as she thought I deserved a week of thinking of nothing else but cycling.

But the happy-go-lucky attitude I was now experiencing came to a sudden end when I was expected to work even further away from home and my day was taken up by driving a five and a half-hour round trip along with the eight hours of time that I was expected to be on site. After a couple of weeks, I was tired and so fatigued that my training was too much for me to even think about and even on weekends I was so tired that my training had dropped dramatically.

Eventually, I was forced by my General Practitioner (GP) to take time from work and 'work-related stress' was quoted as my symptoms, which were more worrying for my doctor, who was concerned about a possible nervous breakdown if I were allowed to continue my work schedule. My company was actually breaking the law by forcing me to drive and work for such long hours each day and though I had suggested it on many occasions – they refused to put me in a hotel to reduce my driving time, I was physically and mentally falling apart.

My unplanned and unwanted break from work was now allowing me to pick up my training and I would go out on my bike every day. I was enjoying my life again but worried about paying my bills – sick pay at work wasn't very much but I was very fortunate to have an understanding and a supportive wife in Angie. Angie was more concerned about my health and to see me suffer was just too much for her to bear – she was happy to see that I was to have a few weeks with no stress and worries about work.

By now, I had finalised the plans for the journey to Montreux and with everything booked and paid for, we just had to wait for the day to come where we would be setting off for Folkestone and the Eurotunnel. Originally, there were to be four of us on the journey but one friend by the name of Clive had to pull out due to family issues, his wife had put her foot down and told him that he couldn't go – this left Andy,

Clint and myself to go on this adventure. Clint owned the local bike shop and Andy worked for him as a bike mechanic in his shop and so I had two experienced bike mechanics on board, from experience of being a regular customer of Clint's – I knew that a cup of tea on this journey would be top notch (as Clint always made a perfect cuppa).

And soon, the day arrived when we had packed up the camper van and were heading for the Eurotunnel in Folkestone and as we were driving on the M5, I just couldn't stop singing 'I LIKE TO CRY AT WEDDINGS' from the sweet charity musical that I was rehearsing with Arcadians musical theatre company.

"For God's sake Glyn, change the bloody record," screamed Clint.

"Let's listen to the radio," added Andy as he reached to turn on the radio.

After a tedious drive along the M40, we had to endure the pain of being on Britain's biggest car park – the M25!

Eventually, we made it to the M20 and Folkestone but on reaching the Eurotunnel terminal, we were to be told that there was a three-hour delay due to people being found in the tunnel at Calais, it seemed that now the UK had voted to leave the EU, there were immigrants with a more determined attitude to find a better life in Britain with some risking their lives in the tunnel and others risking their lives in dinghies on the English channel – made me feel lucky to have the life I have been given.

This delay was to see us arrive in France a little later than expected – we would arrive in the dark hours of the evening and made the decision to drive off the French motorway and park the camper van somewhere and jump into bed for a sleep, I would be able to wake up the following morning and feel fresher and strong enough to take on the roads ahead.

And so, when we eventually reached Calais and drove out of the Eurotunnel terminal, I drove the camper van to a suitable road to park – the night was dark and only the lights of nearby houses were to light our way (lamp-posts were few and far between). After finding a small lay-by, we settled down with a cup of tea (coffee for Clint) before getting into bed and trying to fall asleep. I say trying to fall asleep but due to the fact that when grown men are allowed to go on their own in another country – they become childish and it was no different for us, a chorus of breaking wind and fits of laughter was to be the way to end a tiresome day before eventually falling asleep.

Chapter Seven

Descendre Ma Pelouse
(Get Off My Lawn?)

The next morning, we were woken up with a surprise as someone was banging frantically on the doors and windows of the camper van.

"*DESCENDRE MA PELOUSE. DECENDRE MA PELOUSE!*" came the shouts from the man thumping the side of our vehicle.

"What the hell is that all about?" I shouted to Clint and Andy as I sat up in bed.

"He's shouting something about his lawn," replied Andy who could speak a few different languages.

"GET OFF MY LAWN?" Andy mumbled. "He's telling us to get off his lawn – where have you parked this thing?" he asked as he stared at me.

"I parked in a lay-by I think?" I replied as I was getting dressed.

"You think?" Clint asked. "Don't you know where you actually parked?"

"It was dark last night, lads. I don't know exactly where we parked," I tried to explain as the banging and shouting was getting louder.

"What do you mean by the term 'we parked'?" asked Clint. "You were driving last night, not us," Clint added as he looked at me.

After getting quickly dressed, I was pushed outside by my two mates to face the wrath of a Frenchman who was really angry with us – well me (being as it was me who parked on his lawn).

"*Qui pensez-vous que vous êtes, stationnant sur ma pelouse?*" shouted the Frenchman.

"Queue what?" I asked as I rubbed the sleep from my eyes.

"*Qui pensez-vous que vous êtes, stationnant sur ma pelouse?*" shouted the man again.

"He's asking who do we think we are, parking on his lawn," explained Andy.

"*Désolé monsieur, nous pensions que nous étions garés dans une aire de repos,*" Andy said to the Frenchman.

"I have just explained that we are sorry as we thought we were parked in a lay-by," Andy explained to myself and Clint.

"We are on a charity cycle ride," I tried to explain as I rubbed my thumb against my fingers to signal 'money', but on this, the Frenchman went into a rant.

"What have I said, what have I said?" I asked Andy.

"He thinks you are asking him for money – you idiot!" Andy replied.

"Get back into the van and let me do the talking," Andy demanded as he pushed me back in the van.

83

"*Nous sommes sur un vélo caritatif et arrivons en France assez tard hier soir, nous nous sommes garés par erreur sur votre jardin en pensant que c'était une halte,*" Andy explained to the Frenchman, which I think translated into something along the lines of, "We are on a charity bike ride and parked on your garden by mistake."

So, with a bit of an earlier start to our day than expected, we were now looking for somewhere to get breakfast and after only a few miles (sorry, we were in France and so had to use kilometres), after a few kilometres, we came across a cafe called *'Le Tete Noire'*.

"*TETE NOIRE, TETE NOIRE,*" I screamed in laughter.

"What's funny about that?" asked Clint.

"*Tete noire* is black head in French," I laughed.

"Is it the black head cafe then?" Clint asked as he turned to Andy for an answer.

"Yes, it is," replied Andy. "*Tete* is head and *Noire* is black but in French the words are spelt in reverse."

"So, blackboard is really board black in French," I replied.

"*Tableau noir* should read table or board black but in French its blackboard – *Tete Noire* is really black head in French," Andy went on to explain.

"Well, black head or not, I am starving and going inside for a 'SPOT' of breakfast!" Clint said as he walked through the door with myself and Andy following.

After a good breakfast and an orange juice (they didn't serve English tea), I was getting ready to jump on my bike but drinking a cup of tea (that I made in the van) while I got ready, Clint and Andy checked my bike over and I prepared my drinks bottles before getting on my bike and riding into the distance. My two friends waited a while to allow me to make some distance ahead of them before setting off in the van and so they went back into the 'Black head café' for another cup of coffee.

My plan for the first day was to cycle to Lens, which is 105 km away (63 miles) and my ride along the D119 and the D943 was really quiet roads and made the ride seem like a holiday, it wasn't long before I could hear a loud 'tooting' of a car horn and a vehicle approaching me from behind – it was my support team who were shouting words of encouragement as they overtook me.

Along the way, I came across 'Le Blockhaus d'Eperlecques' which was a museum in a World War 2 military bunker and a great tourist attraction but alas, I had not got time to visit this bunker – my two friends took advantage of visiting the museum which meant that I had overtaken my support van without realising it. I was so pleased that this route that I had chosen was relatively flat and had no real uphill climbs to tackle, the sun was shining and the weather was warm but not over-bearing and I was really enjoying the part of the challenge as the disappointment of the PBP was totally out of my mind.

However, after around twenty-four miles, I stopped to go behind a bush for a wee and when I was in 'mid-stream' I got startled by the blast of a loud car horn which made me jump and caused me to wee down my left leg, the car horn was actually my two mates in the camper van who had caught up with me again.

I was to cycle another four miles before I caught up with my support vehicle, which was parked in a lay-by, my two friends had made a cup of tea which was welcomed at this part of the ride and because I wasn't riding in any event – I was able to have a longer break and two cups of tea instead of one cup. But after examining the road map, we could see that the only hotels in the area were the ones on the motorway service area and so the plan was to ride a couple of hours to an agreed road junction and then I would be driven to the hotel if we weren't to come to a lay-by beforehand. I didn't really want to do this and I was hoping for a lay-by to be on the stretch of road.

After about thirty-seven miles (sixty-four kilometres), I reached a town called 'Aire-De-Sur-Lys' which was in the 'Pas-De-Calais' region of Northern France and had stunning architecture which included 'Collegiale Saint Pierre' a Catholic church that dominated the view of the town. In the town was a beautiful stream like feature that ran through the landscape – it was actually 'Canal D'aire A La Bassee' which had some wonderful landscape and a well-made path along it and after looking at the map, I decided to cycle along this canal path (it looked too beautiful to call it a towpath).

The arrangement was that I cycle along the canal until I reached the D72 and after exiting the towpath, I would cycle along the D72 until I reached a town called 'Beuvry' and then onto the D943 to Lens, where we would rest for the evening. The ride was wonderful and the views along the way were stunning and it was no surprise that I was imagining that I was on the 'PARIS–BREST–PARIS' event for a while and the thoughts of the event were coming to the fore front of my mind.

"Where would I be? Will I still be feeling strong? Will I have reached the finish line?" I kept saying to myself as I cycled along the canal side.

"*Bonjour, belle journée oui,*" called a young lady as she cycled up to me.

"Pardon?" I replied.

"*Bonjour, belle journée oui,*" she repeated.

"Aaah, me English – *Anglais,*" I replied. "*No parle the francais.*"

"*Je ne parle pas francais,*" she laughed in response.

"I was saying that it is a nice day," she repeated.

"A beautiful day and a great one to be cycling," I replied.

"*Oui* – sorry, yes," she replied. "A wonderful day."

"What brings you this far from England on a bicycle?" she asked.

"Oh, my name is Adele," she continued as she introduced herself.

"I am cycling to Switzerland – Lake Geneva, well Montreux to be exact and to visit Freddie Mercury's statue," I explained. "Oh, by the way – my name is Glyn."

"Jim?" she replied in a strong French accent.

"No, Glyn," I repeated.

"Dean?" she replied.

"G-L-Y-N," I spelt out in response as we cycled along.

"Aah, Glen," she replied.

"That'll do – Glen," I smiled back.

Now, anyone who knows me will tell you that my pet peeve are folks who called me Glen by mistake or spelt my name with two Ns, my name was Glyn and not Glynn (of all the Glyns I know, they all had the same pet hates as I did – a kind of Glyn syndrome) but for this young pleasant and pretty French woman, I was only too happy to make an exception.

"How do You expect to cycle all the way through France without being able to speak the language?" she asked.

"I have two friends following me in a van – one of whom speaks French," I explained.

"It's not much good to you if he is in a van somewhere and you are on you own on a bike," she laughed.

"Oui," I replied as if to make myself sound clever.

This part of the ride went really fast as the conversation helped pass away the time and I was to reach Beuvry in great spirits but instead of getting off the canal at the D72 road and into Beuvry – this young lady who was cycling to Beuvry herself (as she lived there) requested that I follow her at a junction of the canal and along a branch of the canal that is called 'La Bas Beuvry'.

This was so much better than cycling on the road, the towpath had views that were mixed with quaint houses and backdrops of beautiful countryside – it was truly stunning and I was seeing a part of France that many holidays makers never get to see.

My two friends were waiting in the town centre for me to arrive (it was so easy to spot them in a camper van that was parked awkwardly in a car park). I approached them in the opposite direction that they expected me to arrive and called out as I got near them.

"*BONJOUR!*" I shouted to my two mates.

"*BONJOUR!*" shouted Adele in unison with me.

"Bloody hell, Glyn's pulled a French bird," laughed Clint.

"Pardon?" asked Adele in her French accent.

"*Glyn a trouvé un ami cycliste*," replied Andy (of which he told me later that it meant 'Glyn had found a cycling friend').

"Aah yes," replied Adele as she turned to Clint. "Glen is very good company, a good man to ride with."

I was dreading the sexual connotation that may come from Clint in response to the word 'riding' but Clint just walked around the other side of the van and silently sniggered away at the thought that I had been 'RIDING' with this girl (riding meant having sex).

Adele helped us order food and drinks in a cafe and of course, I paid for her order as a thank you for her help. As we sat there, she asked Andy to get the maps from the van as she could give me a better and safer route to cycle along than the one I had already plotted.

"*Certaines routes sont trop fréquentées pour faire du vélo,*" she said to Andy.

"Excuse me?" I asked Andy.

"She said that some of the roads that you have chosen are too busy to cycle along," Andy explained.

"I cycle a lot around these parts and I can help keep you safe on these roads," she explained in her very strong French accent.

At this moment, a group of five cyclist walked into the cafe, they were members of Adele's cycling club.

"*Bonjour Adele, qui sont tes amis?*" asked one cyclist.

"*C'est Glen qu'il fait du vélo à Montreux, la statue de Freddie Mercury,*" Adele replied and then explained that her friends had asked who we were and she was telling them of my plans to cycle to Freddie Mercury's statue.

"*Mon cousin habite à Vevey, nonloin de Monteux,*" explained another cyclist.

"He has a cousin who lives in Vevey, near Montreux," Adele translated to me.

"Tenez-moi au courant et je dirai à mon cousin de veiller sur vous lorsque vous arriverez au lac Léman," the cyclist added.

"If you can keep us updated on your progress, he will get his cousin to look out for you," Adele explained.

And after a lengthy conversation between the six, it was decided that Adele would give me her email address and we would keep her and her friends up to date on my progress – more importantly, they wanted to know that I had made it safely.

Adele and her friends helped me chose a few cycling maps from a nearby shop and they marked out routes for me to cycle along, routes that will keep me safer from the traffic and roads that were quieter to cycle along. After saying our goodbyes, I rode away toward Lens in great spirits and the thought that I had made some new friends, however, the logistics of this ride were beginning to worry me – I needed to ride as many miles a day each day to keep myself ahead of the game, if I were to have any issues with my bike along the way, it would add more time to the journey and we had to be finished for the planned date as we all had to be back home in the UK for work and family.

And so, with this in mind, I decided to cycle on as far as I could go before the darkness of the night forced me to stop (or my legs were to start screaming in pain – whichever was to come first). I carried on along roads that had no lamp-posts and as the night began to fall, I was only able to see as far as my bike headlight could allow me to see until eventually, I pulled into a makeshift lay-by and waited for my support team to arrive.

"Are you sure that this is nobody's lawn?" laughed Clint.

I just grinned back as I was now too knackered to reply and with my GPS telling me that I had cycled over ninety-six miles, I was only too pleased to be having a rest. We were near a town called Cambrai.

"Let me have an hour's sleep and I will set off again," I asked my friends.

"You want to carry on?" asked Andy.

"Yes, I have to – if I was on the PBP, I would have to carry on regardless," I explained.

"But this isn't the PBP," Clint said. "Treat this as a holiday and enjoy yourself."

"It's my PBP, it's my PBP-type challenge and anyway – I want to reach Freddie's statue as if I have pushed myself hard to get there and not just wimped my way along, the finish will mean more to me if I have had to push hard to get there," I explained to my friends.

"Look, as we are near a town – why don't we book into a hotel for the night and have a good sleep, God knows we didn't sleep very well last night and were awoken earlier than expected this morning and so a nice comfortable bed is what we need now," Andy stated to me.

"Yes Glyn, with cycling ninety-six miles and riding a 'French woman' you must be knackered," laughed Clint.

"Okay, okay – I could do with a hot shower or a soak in a warm bath anyway," I sighed back to my friends.

"With Adele washing your back?" Clint laughed. "Oooh MONSIEUR GLYN, YOU ARE SUCH A GOOD RIDE – OO LA LA…" Clint continued in a rather convincing French accent.

And so, we booked into a hotel in Cambrai and after a shower we went out for a meal (and boy was I hungry). The town was just like many of the French towns and villages that I had cycled through today – such picturesque places and Cambrai was no different, it had a castle-type building in the middle of a traffic roundabout, it was also located on the junction of the Saint Quentin canal – this town was so beautiful and it was a pity I was too tired to enjoy it more.

After my meal, I went back to my hotel room and just collapsed on my bed which was where I stayed (fully clothed) until the next morning when I was woken up by the banging on my door and the shouts of, "WAKEY, WAKEY" coming from Clint. "Don't be too late for breakfast, mate."

After a quick shower and getting dressed into my cycling gear, I rushed downstairs to the dining room and joined my friends for breakfast – and to my joy, cups of tea!

I was able to have a few cups of tea before setting off on this Saturday morning – it was the yellow label teabags that you get in Europe but it was better than nothing and anyway, I had my box of PG tips in the van for later on – was I happy? You bet I was!

After phoning Angie to let her know I was okay, I set off along the D1044 towards Saint-Quentin and after a good night's sleep, I was feeling refreshed and fully recovered after cycling for a little over two hours and fifteen minutes. I reached Saint-Quentin but instead of stopping for a few photos and some food – I carried on with the attitude of getting as many miles behind me as I can. The day was sunny and the weather was ideal for cycling, very little wind and not too hot – it was as if Mother Nature was willing me along by making the conditions comfortable for this man on a mission.

Back in the van, Andy had emailed Adele with an update and Clint was planning on making a pit stop to check my bike

– this pit stop would be a great chance to grab a bite to eat and have…a cup of tea.

After making a stop in a lay-by, I sat in a deck chair sipping a cup of tea and taking in the views of the surrounding countryside while Clint got busy on my bike.

"You drink a lot of tea," Andy said to me. "Rather a lot."

"It's good for you – tea," I replied as I drank my cuppa.

"In what way?" Andy asked.

"Well, look at me – I am picture of health and beauty, what more proof do you want?" I laughed.

"There's only one thing better than tea – sex," I continued.

"Talking of sex, I wonder how that woman is, the one that says you are a good ride?" laughed Clint as he fiddled away on my bike.

"Did you tell your wife that you had a good ride with a French woman?" asked Clint.

"My Angie is not a jealous wife and I can tell her anything without her getting upset," I declared to my friend.

"But did you tell when you called her this morning?" Clint asked.

"No I didn't – I'll tell her when I get home," I sighed in response.

"Hurry up with my bike," I continued as I tried to change the subject.

The day was ideal and my bike was like riding a new one – I didn't know what Clint had done to it but it was more responsive, the gears were like new and I was able to take on the hills with ease – pity he couldn't do anything about the saddle soreness I was beginning to experience.

I eventually reached Reims in around seven and a half hours which was a round four o'clock in the afternoon and after something to eat (and a cup of tea), I set off again and this time I was going to ride until I couldn't carry on (be it because of my legs becoming tired or the night being too dark), I wanted as many miles behind as possible today.

Reims was eighty-seven miles (according to my GPS) and a steady pace of twelve miles per hour throughout the day, I was still feeling good and able to carry on at the pace I had set myself for the day and so contemplating on reaching one-hundred miles was possible if I were to go for it.

And so, I carried on and counted down each mile as I rode, I really felt like I was in a race today and the attitude of pushing myself had taken over my mind. My speed had quickened and I felt as if I was on one huge mission – I don't know why.

Eventually, I reached a picturesque area of the route that was Montagne de Reims Natural Regional Park and with my GPS indicating that I had cycled 100.1 miles, I decided to call it a day.

I had cycled around eight and half hours but with stops for food and drink (and toilet stops), I had been on the road for almost twelve hours and so we parked the camper van in a wooded car park and settled down for the night.

As I was nodding off to sleep, I could hear the sounds of 'Twit – twoo' bloody owls or something keeping me awake.

"Anybody got a shotgun?" I sighed as I pulled my pillow over my head.

Eventually, we managed to get to sleep but was woken up to the sound of someone screaming. "WHO PUT THAT BLOODY BIKE THERE!" called Clint as he had tripped over my bike.

"I wasn't going to leave it outside the van – someone could have stolen it," I replied as I jumped up in bed.

"Look at my leg, it's gushing with blood," called Clint as he pointed to the cut on his leg.

"Stop being a girlie – put a plaster on it, you'll be alright," I laughed.

"What time is it?" asked Andy as he rubbed his eyes.

"Seven o'clock," I replied.

"Seven o'clock – we have slept for almost ten hours solid," I replied.

"We must have needed it," replied Clint. "Anyway I thought I heard someone sneaking around the van this morning and I was going out to have a look before I got attacked by your bike."

"I'll have a look," I replied as I jumped off my bunk and slipped on a pair of shoes.

I stepped outside and straight away could see a huge wheel clamp on the front wheel.

"Oh, no!" I shouted. "Guys come out here and have a look at this – we've been clamped."

Chapter Eight

Dimanche, Bloody Dimanche
(Sunday, Bloody Sunday)

And so, to our despair, we just stared at the clamp on our van – was this a joke or was it for real?

"Why would anyone want to clamp us?" asked Clint.

"*Pas de stationnement de nuit autorisé* – No overnight parking allowed," called out Andy as he read a nearby sign.

"We didn't see that last night," I replied. "Too dark, I guess."

"What do we do now?" asked Clint.

"Have some breakfast and then I will call the number on the clamp and pay to get the van released," Andy replied. "I parked it so I will pay the fee."

"No way, no way – we will split the fee three ways, mate," Clint replied as I nodded in agreement.

We ate our breakfast and Andy called the number to be released, payment was requested over the phone but Andy wasn't having any of it – payment would be made over the phone when someone was here to release the clamp. It was Andy's fear that we would make the payment and then have to wait all day for someone to come, if we held onto the payment then someone would come out to us sooner rather than later. Thank God! We had someone who could speak French with us – I would have been there for up to a month just trying to explain myself over the phone. However, this was not the best start to the day and despite this issue, we still managed a smile and a giggle about the whole situation.

But in the meantime, I had to get out on my bike and get started on the day ahead, not trying to sound selfish but I had a personal challenge to be getting on with and so it was agreed that I go on ahead and the two friends would catch up with me later.

I cycled along a beautiful tree-lined road and into an area that had vast forests and wetlands and if I wasn't mistaken – vineyards in the distance. I was really enjoying the start to the day (with the exception of the wheel clamp incident). I cycled along a busy but wonderful stretch of the D34 towards Chalons-En-Champagne, which was also lined with beautiful views of wetlands and fields. In just a little over two hours, I had cycled the twenty-four miles (40 km) to Chalons-en-Champagne and it was there that I decided on a drink stop and the chance to phone my dear wife Angie and then my two mates with a wheel clamp issue.

I walked into a cafe and asked to buy a cup of hot water (I had a few teabags in my pocket because I know only too well that I could only buy coffee).

"Excuse me, sir, may I have a cup of hot water?" I asked.

"*Pardon?*" came the reply from the man behind a counter.

"Water – hot water," I replied as the man just stared at me with a puzzled look.

"Aqua, aqua," I replied as I tried to mimic being burned on my hand.

The man shrugged his shoulders and stared at me to indicate that he hadn't a clue what I was talking about.

"Why didn't I do well at school?" I asked myself. "Too much time spent smoking behind the bike shed and not enough time on lessons – that's my problem," I muttered to myself.

But then I had a great idea, I phoned Andy to ask him if the clamp had been released and how to order hot water in French.

"Why would you want to buy hot water in a cafe?" he asked.

"Because I have some teabags and I want to make a cup of tea," I replied.

"You and your bloody tea!" cursed Andy.

"*Eau chaude*," he continued.

"I thought it was aqua, ewe is a female sheep," I replied as Andy hung up.

"*Eau chaude*?" I asked the man behind the counter.

"*Non, vous ne pouvez pas acheter d'eau chaude*," said the man.

I think he was telling that he wasn't going to sell me any hot water – the way he said 'NON' and shook his head gave the game away. I called Andy back to ask for his help and this time I put my phone on loud speaker.

"Mate, tell this bloke that I am willing to pay the same price for the hot water as I would if I was buying a cup of coffee," I asked Andy.

"Just buy a cup of bloody coffee," Andy growled back.

"I don't want a coffee – I want a tea," I snapped back as I could hear Clint laughing his head off in the background.

"*Puis-je acheter une tasse d'eau chaude au même prix qu'une tasse de café?*" Andy shouted over the phone.

"*Oui oui,*" grunted the man behind the counter as he poured some hot water into a mug.

I gladly paid and dangled my teabag in that mug as if I was painting a masterpiece. I took my time to stir the teabag around the white glazed ceramic mug and watch as the water turned to the colour I wanted it to – indicating that my brew was the perfect strength I wanted. And as I placed the used teabag on my saucer, I looked around for the milk – no milk, there was no milk!

I walked up to the counter and asked the man for some milk but he just stared at me in confusion again, so I called Andy again to ask the word for milk in French.

"Hi, mate, how do you ask for milk—" but before I could finish my sentence, "SOD OFF – WE'RE HAVING A CRISIS HERE AND ALL YOU CAN THINK ABOUT IS A CUP OF TEA!"

Then, he hung up.

And so, I was to drink a cup of tea without milk and almost burning my lips in the process, but when it had cooled down, it tasted okay to be honest – the man behind the counter just stared at me, he was probably thinking of how a man could be cycling around the Grand Est region of France without speaking a word of French?

I called Angie to give her an update on the day and thought, stuff Andy, I am not calling him again today – and so I set off again towards Saint-Dizier, which would give me around sixty-five miles in around six hours of cycling.

I rode for about an hour when I got a call from Andy to give me an update on how things were with the van.

"Sorry about earlier mate but I was having a huge issue with the authorities over this clamp," explained Andy. "I had emailed Adele to give her an update on your progress and I had told her what had happened, she asked me to email the details of the company who owned the clamp and she took over from there and sorted the whole thing for us – we are on our way now, where are you?"

"I have gone through Chalons-en-Champagne and on the road to Saint-Dizier," I explained. "Just drive that way and you won't miss me mate."

The weather today was a little unsettled and I had the feeling that I could be encountering some rain during the day but not being a weatherman, I couldn't be certain but the dark clouds that were gathering were cause for concern.

Just as I approached a small village called Vitry-en-Perthois, the heavens opened up and a huge downpour of rain hit me and I was soaked right through before I could put my waterproofs on. I struggled to get my waterproof trousers on and fell over with one leg half in the trousers.

Not realising it at first, but I had gashed my right arm on some decorative rocks that lined the edge of someone's front garden and I jumped around in frustration and cursing the weather at the same time.

"*Excusez-moi monsieur?*" came a voice from behind.

"*Oh – bonjour!*" I replied as I was surprised to see a woman come out in this rain.

"*Es-tu blessé?*" she shouted to me as she tried to make herself heard through the loud crashing noise of the rain hitting parked cars.

"*PARDON?*" I called back.

"*Es-tu blessé?*" she replied.

"*Anglais, je suis anglaise,*" I called back in a bid to tell her that I am English.

"*No parle the old français,*" I went on to tell her.

"*Venez par temps humide,*" she replied as she pointed to her house.

I took this to mean get in from the wet conditions before you catch a cold and I readily followed her up the path. She put my bike in the kitchen and gestured me to take off my wet clothes.

"*Enlève les vêtements et je les sécherai pour toi,*" she said as she pulled at her own clothes to gesture getting undressed.

"*Errm – pardon?*" I whispered in some kind of shock as I was hoping that she was offering to dry my wet clothes (and not suggesting anything sexual).

I was really worried now because being a seasoned cyclist, I wore no underwear beneath my shorts. The padding in cycling shorts were made to be worn next to the skin – the bare bum cheeks and this woman was asking me to take them off.

"*Enlève les vêtements et je les sécherai pour toi,*" she said again as she held her hand out expecting me to hand over my cycling shorts.

I just stood there and wondered how the hell was I going to get myself out of this situation, on that, I turned my back on the woman and pulled my shorts down a little from behind to reveal my bare bum cheeks. "No errm pantalons," I explained.

The woman just laughed and gave me a huge towel to wrap around my modesty and keep all my dignity intact – I was able to get undressed without compromising my reputation (so to speak). The kind lady put my clothes in the tumble dryer and gave me a drink – coffee!

Oh well, it was wet and it was hot and so after emptying my pockets on the settee, I could only wait to see if the rain showed signs of stopping.

I sat there slowly sipping my coffee and watching the rain through the window in the hope it would ease off a little and I could get back on my bike, but just then, I heard the banging of the front door as it slammed shut and a huge man walked into the living room to see me, a naked Englishman sitting on his settee.

"Bonjour, mate!" I nervously said to him as he stormed into the kitchen to confront his wife.

"*Que fait un homme nu dans ma maison?*" he asked his wife, which, I was guessing, he wanted to know what a man with no clothes on was doing in his house?

"*L'homme s'est pris sous la pluie et s'est coupé le bras en tombant,*" she replied as I tried to guess that she was saying that a stupid git fell off his bike in the tipping down of rain.

The man who I had reckoned on being her husband came back into the living room.

"*Où allez-vous à vélo?*" he asked. "Destination?"

"Lake Genève – Lac lumen," I replied as I picked up my phone and showed the man a picture of the Freddie Mercury statue.

"Freddie, Montreux," I added.

"*Cet homme fait du vélo à Montreux!*" he shouted to his wife who was still in the kitchen.

Now, I know that 'Homme' is French for man and Velo is cycle and I presumed that he was telling his wife that I was cycling to Montreux.

Just then, my friends called me on my phone and with my ringtone being the Queen classic 'Don't stop me now' this was to give the man great joy as he sang along to the opening lines. I couldn't help thinking that this man couldn't speak a word of English but yet he could probably recite most of the words to a lot of Queen songs.

I answered the phone to Clint who was now concerned about my welfare and safety but due to loss of signal, he was unable to call me any earlier.

"Mate, get yourself sheltered from the rain and we will pick you up as soon as possible," Clint said with a worried tone in his voice.

"I am in someone's house and her husband has walked in on me sitting half naked in his living room," I explained to Clint.

"Bloody hell! That's another woman you have either been riding with or getting your clothes off for!" laughed Clint.

"Please just get me out of here – soon as you can!" I begged. "Put Andy on the line and he can ask where to pick me up from."

After explaining to Andy the address to collect me from, I sat there and waited with just a towel around me and watched as the rain had now turned into a torrential downpour and it was hitting the windows like nothing I had seen before. In a little over an hour, my friends where knocking at the door and walked into the living room to see me sitting there with a towel around my waist.

"You didn't need a towel to cover up your bits mate – a teabag would have done it," laughed Clint.

"Ask for my clothes – please ask for my clothes so we can get out of here, her husband is freaking me out!"

"*Avez-vous des vêtements de mes amis Madame?*" asked Andy.

"*Je viens de les repasser,*" came the reply from the woman.

"She has almost finished ironing them," Andy called to me.

Bless this wonderful woman who took me in – a complete stranger, and she gave me shelter, a hot drink, warmth and now she was ironing my clothes. I went into the kitchen to get dressed and fumbled my way into my clothes under the shelter of a towel and it felt so good to have warm clothing next to my skin, my bike had left a puddle on the floor of the kitchen but this woman didn't seem to mind. My friends and I eventually said our goodbyes (or our *au revoir*) and left.

The rain was lashing down and the downpour was still torrential and made it obviously too hazardous to cycle in this rain, it was bad enough trying to drive in the conditions but Andy did a good job. I just lay on a bunk and fell asleep for what seemed hours but was in fact around twenty minutes. I was woken up by the louder thumping on the van caused by the rain getting even heavier.

"Bloody hell, it's like a weekend in Wales," I called to my two friends who were sitting in the cab of the van. "Reminds me of holidays in Aberdovey."

"Talking of Wales – your name is Welsh, how's that?" asked Clint.

"I was going to be called Glen but my grandmother, being Welsh, suggested Glyn," I replied.

"I guess Eastwood was behind the reason I was named Clint," laughed my friend.

This started a conversation about our childhood and the things we did as kids, the television programmes we watched and the schools we went to.

"In the early seventies, I was mad on a programme called 'Timeslip' – it was about two school kids who would slip through a time barrier into the past or the future and I would rush home from school to watch it; we didn't have video recorders or TV boxes to record programmes in those days," I reminisced.

"Do you remember the 'Tomorrow people'?" asked Clint. "They were great, they could jaunt by touching their belt buckles and they communicated to each other through telepathy."

"I remember 'The Champions'," recalled Andy. "They had an accident and when they woke up in hospital, they found that they had special powers such as telepathy."

"Yes, I remember 'The Champions', I had a crush on the blonde actress – Alexandra Bastido," I recalled.

"Yes, she was gorgeous – I wouldn't have minded a bit of telepathy with her, sexy conversations and no one could hear us," joked Clint.

This was the topic of conversation all the way to Saint Dizier – our final destination for the day. Today had started bad and got worse but with the driving, I was able to have a longer conversation with Angie (who was really missing me now) and by the time we reached Saint Dizier, we agreed to book into a hotel instead of sleeping in the van. We booked into an Ibis hotel which was basic but great value for money and the luxury of having a nice hot shower was great, a kettle in my room with sachets of coffee was welcoming (especially as I was armed with lots of teabags). I had been emailing friends at home of my progress and they were following me on Google Maps. I had decided not to plot my ride on any social media platform as I didn't want anyone knowing that I had left my wife alone at home as this may have put her in a vulnerable position – someone may have seen it as a chance to break in with little resistance, but then again, my border collie dog would be willing to protect her.

I lay on my bed with my laptop and found a couple of emails from Adele asking how I was and when I was expecting to reach Freddie's statue. I estimated that I would get there by Thursday but why did she want to know?

Her reply was because her cycling friend has a cousin who lived in Vevey not far from Montreux, she was going to arrange a meet with us at Freddie's statue and give me a hero's welcome – this sounded great and added more excitement to the challenge. Because of the day's incident where I found myself alone with a couple of people who couldn't understand me, I decided to download a French language app to my phone which may help me if I needed it.

The next morning, I woke up earlier than expected and had a long hot shower before getting dressed into my cycling gear and after having my breakfast, I sent Andy and Clint a text message that read 'STARTED OUT EARLY – CATCH ME UP LATER ON'.

I set off toward Chaumont which would be around forty-three miles away and I decided not to stop until reached the town, being on my bike I was to take the safer option of cycling along country lanes and away from the direct road to Chaumont but my friends would be able to drive directly on the N67.

The weather had completely changed and was the opposite of the day before, it was warm and sunny – so pleasant to be out cycling on such a day even though this day was to be bit of a tough day with the many hill climbs ahead of me. I reached Chaumont in almost five hours at one o'clock in the afternoon and straight away headed for the nearest cafe.

I didn't bother asking for a cup of hot water to dip a teabag in but instead ordered a croissant and a glass of coke (the caffeine would do me good). As I sat there, I called my friends who told me that they were not far away but to stay there until they had reached me so we could regroup and plan the next stage ahead.

This was going great. The ride and the journey was better than I had thought it would be and apart from the hiccups of the previous day, I was enjoying this immensely. It was Clint's idea to bring a spare bike along in case anything happened to mine on the way and so Andy had bought his bike along just in case it was needed and therefore suggested that he cycle the next leg of the route with me – this was a great idea – to have some company as I cycled was great and so the next leg of the journey was to be fun. Before we set off, I received a phone call from Angie which was a little puzzling.

"Hi, Glyn, can I use your credit card today?" she asked.

"May I ask what for?" I replied.

"An unexpected bill has come in and I need to pay it," she explained.

"Well, it is there for emergencies, so why not?" I told her.

Now, I am lucky to be married to a completely honest and trustworthy woman and I can tell when Angie is not being completely truthful – she is totally hopeless at telling lies. The reasons for her wanting to lie to me were probably because she was planning a surprise in some way – perhaps a celebratory party for when I get home but I knew that she was up to something, bless her.

From Chaumont I cycled with Andy as a companion and we headed toward Langres, which was another twenty-five miles away (or 40 km). The route was nice but with a few uphill climbs – the time was spent with me having a few lessons in the French Language from Andy, learning French and cycling – there's a novelty.

"*Puis-je avoir une tasse de thé?* Can I have a cup of tea?" Andy called out as he cycled alongside me.

"*Push a vor une tassle de te?*" I replied.

"No, it's – *Puis-je avoir une tasse de thé?*" repeated Andy.

"What's the use of trying to order a cup of tea in French anyway? They only drink bloody coffee," I replied after many attempts to repeat what Andy was asking me to say.

But I will admit that every road sign we saw along the way, Andy would read it out to me and I would repeat it back, this made the next twenty-five miles pass quickly and we reached Langres in two and half hours and as the time was four o'clock in the afternoon, I considered this as too early to retire for the day and wanted to press on ahead.

I had cycled for almost sixty-eight miles now (almost eight hours of cycling) and with the thought that the roads ahead were to become more hilly; I wanted to make good progress now in case I hit a few tough spots later on in the challenge, after a bite to eat and a cup of tea – I headed off once more but this time on my own as Andy was to take over from Clint as driver.

I rode out with my support van ahead of me and they would pull into lay-bys when they could and wait for me to catch them up. I was cycling really well on this part of the route but looking at my GPS I could see that this was a slightly downhill road for many miles ahead. Taking advantage of the downhill road, I was able to pedal and then roll along the road which was helping me stay comfortable on the bike, but eventually the sun started to set and it was becoming dusky – I was beginning to feel tired. I reached a town called Gray and what a stunning town, so like many towns I had cycled through – wonderful architecture and beautiful landscapes, I decide to stop here for the night.

Clint managed to ask a local about the best place to park the camper van even though he didn't speak French, a moment of body gestures and a game of charades took place as Clint gestured about the van, putting his hands to his face in a sleeping gesture must have made the local think that we needed to park up and get some sleep and though it would have been quicker to get Andy to ask – Clint did a great job, for this man gave us what looked like a parking permit to allow us to park along the river. I had now cycled almost one-hundred miles in twelve hours (that included the drink stops I had) and it was now approaching 7:30 in the evening and I was bloody tired – so tired that I didn't go out for anything to eat, a bag of crisps and a chocolate bar was enough for me to eat before going to bed and get ready for Tuesday – the following day.

Chapter Nine

Besancon to Lausanne

Tuesday was looking such a wonderful day as I woke up in a positive mood. Though my legs were stiff, I was still able to get myself motivated, my two friends had worked out a plan – if I were to cycle to Besancon and then onto Pontarlier, I could then cross the border into Switzerland and ride on to Lausanne on Wednesday which would give me a very short distance to ride on the Thursday morning when I reached Freddie's statue.

The plan for Tuesday was to ride around sixty-five miles to Ponterlier and call it a day no matter how fit I may still be feeling. After having a cup of tea and a chocolate bar, I set off yet again ahead of my support team who were still in bed. I was cycling to Besancon which was thirty-one miles away – an easy thirty-one miles or so I thought!

The terrain on this part of the ride was tough and relentless as the roads went up and down like a tarmac rollercoaster and I was now finding this challenge really tough, doubts started to come into my head.

"Had I pushed too hard at the start of the challenge?" I kept saying to myself. "Had I cycled too far yesterday?"

I decided that today was to be an easy day and forgot about riding at 12-14 miles per hour, I would settle for ten miles per hour and rest my tired legs for the day. I had been cycling for around an hour when I came to a mobile cafe in a lay-by and yet again, I was going to try to order a cup of hot water for my teabag. The poor young woman who was serving me tried so hard to understand me but was having no success. I got my phone out and opened the French app – frantically, I looked for anything that resembled ordering a cup of tea (oh I wished I had listened to Andy a little better yesterday).

The list of phrases on this app was things like, "How do I get to the beach?", "Where's the nearest post office?" and "Where's the nearest hospital?"

And so, I dangled a teabag in front of me and gestured that I want a cup of tea.

"*Aah je vois – thé,*" she replied as she reached for a yellow label 'breakfast teabag'.

Oh joy, I was getting a cup of tea – okay it was the weak kind of teabag you got when you ventured outside of the UK, but I could top it up with one of my own teabags and make it a decent cuppa. I just sat down on one of the white plastic chairs that was there for customers and drank that tea like it was the last cuppa on earth and because I had left the van early this morning, I had ordered me a bacon sandwich (well on the menu it said 'sandwich au bacon'). I had completely drank my first cup of tea before my sandwich was ready and so I ordered another cup of tea but as the young lady reached for another yellow label teabag – I offered her one of mine and she put that in my mug instead.

As I sat there munching on my sandwich, my two friends pulled into the lay-by and were laughing at the sight of me just chilling out at a roadside cafe.

"That's a picture of a dedicated athlete," said Clint as he took a photograph of me.

"Healthy eating – a bacon sandwich is that mate?" he asked as he was videoing me.

"The best way to start the day." I said as I continued munching on my sandwich.

Clint and Andy ordered the same but with a cup of coffee and as they waited for their orders, I decided to set off again after making plans to meet up in Besancon.

As I set off, my mind was pleasantly distracted by the stunning views and scenery of the route. I could see a river in the distance and hills that dominated the skyline. Each town and village I had the good fortune to cycle through was like going back in time as the buildings were standing so boldly and prominent (as they had done for many years previously).

I reached Besancon in four and half hours – a slow time to be honest but I wasn't bothered, today was all about enjoying the ride and allowing my aching legs to recover. Besancon is a beautiful city near the border with Switzerland. The old city centre lay on the Doubs River. The Citadel of Besançon was on a hill and was home to museums and a zoo. At the foot of the hill, Besancon Cathedral had a unique 70-dial astronomical clock that indicated sunrise and sunset, eclipses, and tides in French ports.

I met up with my support team and we decided to have a look around the city for an hour as this would give me time to stretch my legs and the chance to take in the beauty of the place. I couldn't believe just how wonderful the city was – and again, the architecture was simply amazing.

It was now one o'clock in the afternoon and I had to focus on getting to Pontarlier which was another thirty-two miles away and so I was setting off on my bike once more.

The time spent walking around Besancon had really helped to ease the aches in my legs and this was evident in the speed I was now riding my bike, but this wasn't going to last too long as the roads got steeper and steeper, my speed got slower and slower and I was not enjoying the day.

I met my support team in a lay-by and as they saw me approaching in the distance, they had a cup of tea waiting for me. I sat down and stretched out my legs while Clint gave my bike another service. Andy offered me the option of jumping into the van but I refused the offer. I was on a journey that was so special to me – as a fan of Queen, I wanted to make a huge gesture to my hero Freddie Mercury by taking on the most gruelling challenge to reach his statue and so I was cycling all the way (unless adverse weather conditions were to threaten my safety).

I cycled onto Pontarlier and the pace was agonisingly slow due to the constant uphill climbs but when I reached the town, I was yet again amazed at the beauty of the buildings – I cycled through the 'Triumphal arch of the Porte Saint-Pierre' (St. Peter's Gate) a huge arch that dominated my view from miles ahead. I was totally knackered but totally blown away by the views that greeted me in Pontarlier.

It was getting dark and this indicated a tough day of cycling for me as the shorter distance had taken me longer to cover – sixty-five miles in twelve hours was really poor for a man like me and even though I had stopped more times than the days previously, it read as a bad at the office – or a bad day in the saddle.

It was too late to try and find a hotel so we parked up the van and settled in for the night, I was so fatigued that all I could manage was some soup and as before – the shower in our van was not heating up the water correctly which meant a slightly warm shower instead of a hot one, but it was better than nothing. I looked at the map for the following day and could see that the route to Lausanne in Switzerland was going to be another tough day.

I woke up the next day without that enthusiasm that I had on the previous days 'Wimping Wednesday' I was calling today – as I felt like a wimp who was giving in to all his aches and pains. I sat in the van and was eating my breakfast while Clint had popped out to get me some muscle rub for my legs, Andy had advised him to try and find a tub of 'Emu oil' as it would the best thing for me at this moment in time. Clint came back with the tub of emu oil and a barrage of swear words as well.

"This small tub cost the equivalent of twenty-five pounds – twenty-five quid for this little tub," Clint ranted.

"I'll give you the money back," I said to Clint.

"No worries mate – I used your wallet anyway, you've already paid for it," he grinned back at me.

Andy got to work and massaged my legs with this expensive oil but within a few seconds I could feel the heat penetrating my legs and easing into my muscles, this was taking away all my aches and pains and before long I felt like I had a new pair of legs and I was now ready and eager to jump on my bike. I rode out of Pontarlier in a positive frame of mind and I had one thing in mind – to reach the top of the highest peak before cycling the downhill road into Lausanne.

Today was going to be a forty-mile ride in total but the climb across the border into Switzerland was going to prove very challenging – this was going to be tough as I was to tackle the mountains ahead of me and so I cycled away under a huge cloud of anticipation. As I cycled out of Pontarlier, it wasn't long before I realised that my route was now also shared with the N57 – a motorway!

I stopped and reached for my pocket maps and plotted a route on my GPS, these were small routes of around ten-mile in each section and would navigate me around the motorway system, eventually I reached a town called 'Mouthe', which was eighteen miles from Pontarlier and on reaching there, I plotted my next section.

The next destination was a town called Mont-la-Ville in Switzerland and it was on this fifteen-mile section that I would cross the border from France, I had been cycling for over four hours now and had covered thirty-five miles of what should have been a forty-mile bike ride – thirty-five miles and Lausanne was still twenty miles away.

I was totally shattered by the time I had reached Monte-la-Ville, the constant uphill climb to the top of this mountain was so exhausting and so cold too, but the low part of this ride was cheered up by the site of life-size plastic cows that were painted red with a white cross on them – Switzerland cows. By now, the effects of the emu oil was wearing off and my legs were beginning to ache again but this could have been down to the fact that I had cycled constantly up a huge mountain and punished my legs in the process. I calculated that my next part of the ride would be a mainly downhill ride into Morges and then along the roads that follow the Lake and into Lausanne.

The next section was great as a downhill ride was ahead of me – well, I say ride, more like rolling downhill and resting my legs. The views were breath-taking and the roads so great to be riding on, I could see Lake Geneva in the distance and the beauty of the surrounding mountains that gave it a most stunning backdrop. The closer I got to Morges, the better the view and I just couldn't believe that such a place of beauty even existed on this planet – I could understand why Freddie Mercury fell in love with the place. In 1978, Queen released their seventh studio album that was titled 'JAZZ' and it was recorded in Mountain studios, Montreux and it was at this time that Freddie Mercury fell in love with Montreux.

The Freddie Mercury statue being in Montreux and not London is a mystery, to be honest, the decision to erect the statue here seemed logical enough being as the mountain studio was here but all the stars that had graced Wembley from football to music – nobody dominated the stadium in a way that Freddie did and so to have Freddie Mercury's statue dominating the view outside of Wembley would be justified, however, to have a great reason to visit Lake Geneva such as visiting Freddie's statue was a great excuse to be here.

I reached Morges and stopped for a drink and bite to eat. I was unaware that my two support mates were trying to contact me but as I had no signal on my phone, they kept going straight to my voicemail. This was a worry to the pair who had expected to see me along the way and then panicked when they realised that part of my planned route was now a motorway.

When I eventually obtained a signal, I called my friends and I explained the change of plan and gave them an estimated time of arrival of which they informed that they had booked us into an Ibis hotel and they would be waiting for on the waterfront in Lausanne.

I checked my GPS and could see that I was less than an hour away from Lausanne and the end of this challenging day of cycling, I just kept a look out to the lake as I couldn't believe that one body of water could be so vast – it was simply breathtaking (a word I had used lot recently but I just couldn't put it into words how stunning this place was). I cycled towards Lausanne and just soaked in the atmosphere and the surrounding beauty as I rode along.

I eventually reached Lausanne and my two friends on the waterfront of the city and again this was so beautiful – 'Place de la navigation' had a man-made 'stream' going along the esplanade with fountains of water shooting into the air, modern metal constructed bridges that went over the stream. Children were playing and laughing in the water and families were being proper families as they joined together in the fun.

I felt really blessed to be here in this place, it was like a different world and it lifted the aches and pains in my legs as I felt a whole sense of achievement take over my body.

We had to meet a friend of Adele's at the 'Parc Olympique' or Olympic park to us British folk. This athletic park had some wonderful statues such as a group of athletes holding up the five rings of the Olympic flag, a great cycling monument and the Olympic-themed statues.

We met a man on a Harley Davidson motorbike who did speak a little English and went out of his way to make sure that we understood what he was saying. I asked him if he wanted to swap his bike for mine (even though mine hadn't got an engine) and he laughed in acknowledgement that I was joking.

"Okay, the plan for tomorrow is that you get to Vevey in your own time and you will meet up with me and a few friends and we will plan on how to get you to Montreux safely."

I did think that this was strange that he was concerned about me cycling the short distance from Vevey to Montreux, after all, I had cycled across France and into Switzerland with no worries or concerns but I went along with it as I didn't want to appear ungrateful for his kind offer.

After a coffee and a long chat with the guy, we set off to the hotel (a steep walk up to the city centre) and while Andy was putting my bike in the van, I was having a nice warm shower. Clint was in my room and making me a cup of tea ready for when I got out of the shower – I got dressed and sat on my bed, looking out at the scenery that dominated the view from my bedroom.

"I could live this life – most definitely I could live here," I called over to Clint.

"Fancy owning a bike shop here mate," replied Clint.

"Not just a bike shop but water sports, team sports – hey with me being a dodgeball coach, I could open up a dodgeball section within the shop," I stated as I was letting my imagination get carried away with me.

"Who's opening up a dodgeball shop?" asked Andy as he walked into my room.

"A sports shop for anything sporty," I replied.

"Well, before that, are we going out for a meal?" Andy asked.

"Will you rub some emu oil in my legs before we go mate?" I asked Andy, of which he agreed.

We went out shopping and as I was raised with five sisters, I thought that I had been programmed with the shopping gene over the years and this was evident as I was running in and out of shops and stores and though prices were more expensive around here – I still couldn't resist buying myself a few things and for Angie, of course.

We went into a restaurant and ordered some food, and as we waited for our order to come to our table, we had a great chat about the journey so far.

"It'll all be over tomorrow," said Andy. "Are you pleased?" he added as he looked at me.

"Yes and no," I replied. "Yes I am pleased that I have that distance out of the way but no I don't want it to be over just yet – I am enjoying this, being here."

"Tomorrow, you will be achieving your goal in Montreux," added Clint. "How are you feeling about that?"

"Oh God, I am so excited – do you know the feeling that you get when butterflies are in your stomach?" I replied. "That's how I am feeling now, it means that much to me."

"I have told you that I have a replica of the Freddie Mercury statue at home," I asked my two friends. "It's a pewter figure on a black plinth and stands about twelve to fifteen inches tall."

"Such a great fan then?" asked Andy.

"Yes, I am but there are many folks out there who are bigger fans than me," I explained.

The conversation went on for quite a while with all the highs and lows of the past few days – the wheel clamp, meeting Adele and her friends and me trying to order a cup of hot water, it seemed like weeks ago rather than a few days previously but here we were talking about the final day – tomorrow when I get to pay the greatest tribute to my hero – Freddie Mercury.

I tried to get to sleep but I just kept tossing and turning in my bed, it got so bad that I got up and made myself a cup of tea – I was like a little child who was excited on Christmas eve and waiting for Santa Claus to arrive. This seemed so silly and to many folks, it would be a case of visiting a statue – but this wasn't just any statue, it was my all-time hero – the man who kept me sane through the bad days of 1977 when I was diagnosed with epilepsy.

In 1977, I was confined to the house for my own safety and therefore, I had confined myself to my bedroom with my record player and my Queen LP's and I definitely did feel that Freddie was my only friend through teenage nights (just as it said in the song 'Radio Ga Ga') and so finding Freddie tomorrow was my own personal way of saying thank you to the hero I never got to meet.

I sat on the edge of my bed as I sipped my tea and recalled my past, well, the year of 1977, a bad year – a year when I lost my pet dog, I lost my grandmother and I lost my independence that year too. I could never think of 1977 without tears in my eyes and this evening was no different as I remembered that year. At a time when I was just fourteen years old, I could have thought of death being a kindness to me, but instead, I dreamed of owning the stage, commanding a huge audience and being the best frontman a band could ever have – I dreamt of being like Freddie and this dream kept me sane and helped me to focus on things beyond the epilepsy that I was going through at the time – thanks Freddie.

I dried my eyes and managed to get to sleep eventually.

Chapter Ten

Finding Freddie Mercury

I woke up the next morning and I had totally lost track of time and I found it difficult to even recall what day it was and I had to look at my watch to see that it was Thursday – and yes, I got my prediction correct that I would reach Freddie's statue on Thursday. Andy had been emailing Adele on her friends and I trust that he had told them that I was on schedule for making that day as predicted.

At breakfast, I went through the plans for the day with Clint and Andy and with Vevey being eleven and a half miles away, I was safe to predict an hour of cycling and instructed my two friends to call our friend in Vevey with an estimated time of arrival as soon as I left on my bike.

I had only got fifteen and a half miles to cycle today and I was able to be more relaxed for the day and planned to set off at nine o'clock and reach Vevey at ten o'clock, Andy asked if he could cycle the last day with me and I was only too pleased to have him cycle with me.

And so, we set off at nine o'clock and rode along the route de Lausanne toward Vevey, the day was pleasant and so bright and sunny – the roads were remarkably clean with no litter thrown from vehicles. The views of the lake as we rode along was just so fantastic and we could see lots of activities taking place in different areas around the lake – it was great.

Andy was (as always) great company and a good companion to cycle with and the conversation covered anything and everything from politics to science to fitness, we were just passing away the time and enjoying this final day of cycling. Andy was asking about the reason I became such a big fan of Queen and why was Freddie Mercury such a huge part of my life and so I told him my story of the year 1977.

"I was just a fourteen-year-old kid without a care in the world. I was earning my own money by delivering newspapers for a local newsagent – I even saved up enough money to buy myself a bike," I recalled as we rode along. "1977 was a year that is burned in my memory forever, the upset of my dog dying followed by the trauma of losing my grandmother and when I thought that things couldn't possibly get any worse – I was diagnosed with epilepsy. I couldn't leave the family home alone and would need a chaperone if I wanted to go anywhere but as only family members knew of my condition, I could only rely on my brother or my sisters to escort me to anywhere I needed to go – it wasn't right to expect my sisters to have the responsibility of a brother who could have a seizure at any given time while in their care and so I never went out – Mum and Dad were always at work but they would take the family out at weekends but apart from that, I stayed confined to my bedroom with only my record player for company. It was then when I realised that I had every single that Queen had released among my record collection and I would play them over and over – before long I had the back catalogue of Queen LP's and I would pre-order any Queen LP's in the future," I explained to Andy.

"Do you know that I had three seizures on my paper round – alone in the middle of roads and streets before anyone witnessed me in a seizure?" I told Andy as I was getting tearful and on that, we pulled over to the side of the road as I started to cry.

"I am sorry mate but 1977 was so bad for me that I am reduced to tears when I think of that year – it changed my life completely, my life had taken a different path because of the jobs I was unable to apply for because of epilepsy – I couldn't even hold an HGV licence," I sobbed to my mate.

"Could you pretend it never happened and just block the whole year from your memory?" asked Andy.

"I am on medication for life to control epilepsy, so each morning I have a reminder of 1977 as I take my pills, my grandmother dying really hit me hard and I still miss her now – forty-two years later and I miss her still," I sighed as I fought back my tears. "I think that she was part of the reason I have achieved so much as an ultra-distance runner because when I crossed the finish line of a 150-mile race or I had broken a world record for running on a treadmill –I would always think that my grandmother was looking down on me and being so proud of what I had done."

I said as I looked up to the sky.

We had our chat disturbed by a loud and frantic tooting of a car horn – it was Clint approaching us from behind and a final blast of the horn as he drove away in the distance.

The weather was getting hot and we cycled on to a petrol station forecourt to buy two small bottles of coke that were nice and chilled from a refrigerator, it was here that I had noticed that Andy was wearing a Bluetooth ear piece (something that he had never done before while riding a bike) but he told me that he was expecting a call and didn't want to hold me up by having to stop and answering it.

We reached Vevey and cycled to 'AILE CASTLE, Chateau-del'aile' where we were met by a gang of eight Harley Davidson owners – I just stood there speechless as I looked at each and every motorbike, these guys are to give me an escort to Montreux and it was all arranged between Andy, Clint and Adele.

"What the f—?" I asked as I tried to process what was going on.

"You will arrive at Freddie's statue in style," replied Clint.

"These guys will ride behind us and give us a hero's welcome into Montreux," Andy added.

I was even more excited than ever, having a Harley Davidso escort to Montreux was just amazing and something I wouldn't have even dreamed about, I was totally gobsmacked but in a good way. Clint had set off ahead of us so he could find somewhere to park the van and have time to meet us at the statue for when we arrived.

We cycled along the Quai Perdonnet road and onto the Rue d'entre-deux Villes road (according to the road sign), along the Route de Saint-Maurice, we were closer to the lake and it was beautiful views when suddenly Andy was talking French into his Bluetooth ear piece, he was just chatting away until suddenly…a group of cyclists came from nowhere and joined us on our ride, it was Adele and her cycling club who had been planning with Clint and Andy to join me today for the final part of the challenge. What a day, what a day – myself, Andy, a group of cyclists and a few Harley Davidson motorbikes on a road alongside Lake Geneva and no other driver seemed bothered to try to overtake us, it was a great moment.

"*Bravo, bravo…le maintenir,*" shouted a few of my fellow cyclists, which I translated as well done.

This moment was reminiscent of a scene from a Rocky film but instead of running up some concrete steps, I was cycling along a road from Vevey to Montreux and I was beginning to get emotional at this point (luckily, I was wearing my cycling shades and nobody could see my eyes watering).

Just then a police car pulled up in front of us and made us stop, two officers got out of the car and while one officer directed the traffic around us, the other was talking to the group of bikers.

"*Qu'est-ce qui se passe ici?*" asked the officer as I assumed he was asking what was happening.

"*Accompagner un cycliste caritatif à Montreux, Officier,*" replied one of the bikers as I sat on my bike bemused by the situation.

"He's telling the officer that you are having an escort to Montreux," explained Andy.

"*Officier, cet homme a parcouru l'Angleterre, la France à vélo pour se rendre à Montreux et visiter la statue de Freddie Mercury,*" interrupted Adele as she explained to the officer.

"She explaining that you have cycled from England to get to Montreux and visit Freddie Mercury's statue," Andy explained and on that, a second police car pulled up.

The first officer walked up to me and looked me up and down and as he walked around me and my bike, "*Savez-vous que vous pouvez provoquer une obstruction?*" asked the officer.

"Do you know that you are causing an obstruction?" Andy translated.

"What's the word for sorry?" I asked Andy.

"Pardon," Andy replied.

"I asked, what's the word for sorry?" I replied again.

"PARDON!" Andy called back to me.

"Have you gone bloody deaf? I was asking—" I began to explain as Andy interrupted.

"The word for sorry is pardon," he bellowed at me.

"*Cet homme était censé faire du vélo sur l'événement Paris–Brest–Paris mais malheureusement il ne pouvait pas le faire et il a donc décidé de faire du vélo à Montreux à la place*," Adele explained to the police officer.

"You were supposed to be cycling on the Paris–Brest–Paris event but unfortunately you couldn't do it and so you decided to cycle to Montreux instead," Andy translated to me once more.

"*Alors tu es fan de Queen, Freddie Mercury hein?*" asked the first officer as I stared back in total confusion.

"He's asking if you are a fan of Queen, Freddie Mercury?" explained Andy.

"Of course I am a bloody fan – I wouldn't have cycled this far if I wasn't," I whispered back to Andy.

"*Oui, oui – l est fan de Queen,*" Andy replied on my behalf.

"*Vous voulez faire du vélo, vous voulez faire du vélo,*" the officer sang – in a fashion.

"You want to ride your bicycle – you want to ride your bike?" Andy said with a puzzled expression.

"Yeah, I recognised the tune but he ain't no Freddie," I replied.

The officer went over and started talking to the other three officers and as we stood there, we were seriously thinking that we would be charged with some traffic offence and I would be halted from completing my challenge – just two miles from Freddie Mercury's statue and I would be stopped, I just hung my head in disappointment.

"*Je conduirai devant vous, mes collègues conduiront derrière vous et nous vous donnerons un passage sûr vers votre destination,*" called the officer as he walked to his car.

"WE ARE GETTING A POLICE ESCORT!" shouted Andy and Adele in unison.

"*Parce que vous avez moins de trois kilomètres à parcourir, nous pouvons vous accompagner pendant votre voyage,*" shouted the second officer.

"We only have three kilometres (two miles) to go and so we can be allowed to carry on – with a police escort too," Adele explained.

What a day – and what a way to end a challenge, a police car with flashing lights ahead of me and a group of cyclists behind with a group of Harley Davidsons behind them and a police car at the back flashing his lights. The final two miles were to be the best part of this challenge.

Eventually, we could see Montreux in the near distance and my stomach was experiencing more and more butterflies, passers-by and other motorists had assumed that because of my cortege of followers, I was on a charity bike ride and tooted their car horns in celebration of my achievement – 'Bravo' came the shouts from pedestrians as I cycled past.

I cycled along the main road that went through Montreux with my group alongside me until we saw a turning to my right – 'Place du Marche' a small road that was access to the promenade to the lake and at the bottom of 'Place du Marche' was Freddie Mercury's statue overlooking the grand view of the lake. I sprinted to the statue and slowly got off from my bike, as I was met by Clint. I just handed him my bike as I walked around the front of the statue. I stood there for what felt like ages and just stared up at Freddie.

My escort group and I surrounded the statue along with a group of tourists and we were all in awe of this magnificent figure that had captured Freddie in his most famous pose, I walked around the statue a couple of times and then I just stared at the front of Freddie. This was an unforgettable moment in my life and I only wish that my wife was here to share it with me (she is a fan too and has Freddie Mercury's 'I was born to love you' as her ringtone on her phone). I touched Freddie's statue and ran my hand around the figure as I walked around him again. I couldn't believe that I was here as it was like meeting the man himself in person.

I looked up at the statue and recalled my childhood, a childhood blighted by epilepsy in a period when the subject was never talked about in public (unlike the understanding attitude of society in today's times). I thought back to those days when I was banned (for my own safety) from riding my bike and from swimming – my pastime was really restricted but my days were less tedious thanks to Queen…Brian May, John Deacon, Roger Taylor and of course – FREDDIE MERCURY.

All thanks went to my wonderful family for pulling through the worse year of my life, that year of epilepsy but Queen and Freddie played a part too.

As I stood there, I could hear Clint talking to a few bystanders.

"He even has Queen's 'Don't stop me now' as his ringtone," Clint was telling a tourist. "Talking of phones – have you called Angie?" Clint added as he looked at me.

"My wife, my wife – in all of the excitement I forgot to ring Angie to let her know that I have done it," I called out as I fumbled for my phone.

Retrieving my phone from the saddle bag of my bike, I quickly dialled my wife's number that was obviously stored on my phone and I waited for the dealing tone... 'I WAS BORN TO LOVE YOU' came the sound of someone's ringtone from behind me.

"That's the same as my wife's ringtone!" I called as I turned round.

Standing in front of me was Angie who was (as always) emotional as she ran up to me and hugged me so tight, we were both in floods of tears as we whispered, "Missed you," to each other.

"So, this is what you wanted to use my credit card for?" I asked in a joking manner.

"Sorry – but I have max'd your card," she replied.

"Don't worry – it's worth it," I sighed in reply.

We both stood with our arms around each other and stared at Freddie's statue, we just stared for what seemed ages and by now the huge crowd that was here earlier was getting smaller until only the group of cyclists were with us.

Adele and her friends were to be taking a train to Lausanne and then on to Besancon, from Besancon they would be cycling home (a twenty-hour ride), I thanked them for their support before waving goodbye and Angie also thanked them for being so kind towards me.

"Right, follow me," Clint asked. "I have a surprise for you."

We followed him for a short walk to the Casino Barriere and the studio where Queen had recorded the album 'JAZZ'. This was amazing – it was full of memorabilia such as Freddie's stage costumes and concert tickets (of which I had many myself). A round brass plate that was screwed to the floor had the words 'Freddie Mercury stood here when he sang his last song – Mother love'. I knelt down and touched it, rubbing my hand over the brass plate I looked up to Angie, "He will never be replaced – Freddie, there will never be another performer like him," I said with a lump in my throat as Angie agreed.

This studio experience was open to all of the public and was free to enter, visitors were welcome to donate money or any spare coins if they wished and all donations went to the Freddie Mercury Phoenix Trust (Phoenix being on the emblem of the Queen crest).

After a memorable visit to the studio experience, we were making our way to the hotel. Angie had booked a one-way ticket to fly to Geneva and was travelling home with us in the van the next day – it was the first time in a week that I would be sleeping in the same bed as my wife but I would probably be too tired to take advantage of the situation. As we walked back to the hotel, we stopped at a shop that sold everything Swiss, even cuckoo clocks and Angie insisted that we go in, it was a fantastic shop that also sold items connected to Queen.

The owner was to tell us that he had an agreement with Brian May and Roger Taylor (Queen Productions Ltd) that he would sell items in his shop and not on the internet, this was for the true fans of Queen who had made the journey to Freddie's statue. As I was talking to the shop owner, Angie was calling for the attention of a shop assistant who opened a glass cabinet and handed her an item of jewellery to look at. I walked over to see what she was doing – Angie was examining an 18-carat gold Freddie Mercury pendent which was a small replica of the statue outside. Because of its value the shop owner could not afford to stock these pendants and so it was the only one he had.

"Would you wear this if I bought it for you?" Angie asked.

"I would but it's too expensive," I replied.

"It's not as expensive as the bill I have given you on your card for flying out here and booking a room for the night," Angie said.

And so, it was bought, this 'one-off' Freddie Mercury pendent that I would wear with pride.

We woke up the next morning but instead of having breakfast in the hotel, we decided to buy a coffee (I had taken a teabag with me) and some food and go back to see Freddie's statue one last time before we left Montreux.

We sat on the wooden construction that is the 'Platorme sur le lac' and just stared at the statue as we pondered on the fact that the figure had captured everything about Freddie, even the way Freddie dominated his audience with his charm and personality was captured in the statue.

We were joined by Andy and Clint who had seen us leave the hotel and as we sat there Andy commented.

"Seven days, seven days to get here," he said.

"You set out on last Friday and got here yesterday – Thursday," added Clint as he counted the days on his fingers.

I gave out a little laugh as my wife looked at me with a puzzled expression which indicated that she didn't understand what I was laughing at.

"In only seven days – a song on the Jazz album, Queen's Jazz album," I told my friends.

"*I never thought that this could happen to me, in only seven days,*" I sung as I looked at Freddie's statue.

It was time to head off home and with a few days of driving ahead of us, we wanted to leave as soon as possible, it was a difficult thing to do by walking away from that statue as I wished that I could have had a little more time to stay in Montreux. I walked around Freddie's statue and again, I rubbed my hand on the figure as I walked around – I made a promise to myself; this may be the first time I had visited Freddie's statue but it wouldn't be the last.